The Dark Moon

Anne Maria Clarke

related books by
Archive Publishing

Her Blood is Gold *Lara Owen*
A Twist in Coyote's Tale *Celia M. Gunn*
Performing the Dreams of your Body *Dr. Jill Hayes*

and in the 'Wisdom of the Transpersonal' series by
Ian Gordon-Brown and *Barbara Somers*
Series Editor *Hazel Marshall*

Journey in Depth: A Transpersonal Perspective
The Fires of Alchemy: A Transpersonal Viewpoint
The Raincloud of Knowable Things:
A Practical Guide to Transpersonal Psychology

other titles distributed by Archive by
Bryce Taylor
Working with Others
Forging the Future Together
Learning for Tommorrow: Wholeperson Learning

for full details please see our website

www.archivepublishing.co.uk
and
transpersonalbooks.com

The Dark Moon

Anne Maria Clarke

Editor
Hazel Marshall

Illustrations and cover design
Ian Thorp

ARCHIVE
publishing

2008

First published in Great Britain by
Archive Publishing
Wimborne Dorset England

Designed for Archive Publishing by Ian Thorp

© 2008 Anne Maria Clarke

The rights of Anne Maria Clarke as author
have been asserted in accordance
with the Copyright, Designs and Patents Act 1988.

A CIP Record for this book is available from
the British Cataloguing in Publication data office

ISBN 978-1-906289-05-8   Hardback
ISBN 978-1-906289-04-1   Paperback

Printed and bound in Latvia by
Dardedze Holography

PREFACE

Sometimes only poetry will do; sacred words, sacred songs striking into the hearts of all that hear. Such pages of poetry, and the myths and fairytales that were to become the central barometers of the search for my lost child, were where I found most solace, most insight, most medicine for my pain; because nothing else – and I read a good deal of 'the literature' on these matters – touched so profoundly upon what I was experiencing, and nothing else more clearly pointed a way home. My wish is that through tracking my own journey through several years of darkness, you too may find comfort and renewed hope.

DEDICATION

The Dark Moon is for everyone affected by the issue of child sexual abuse, but mostly it is for our own beautiful daughter. A message – in a bottle, if you like – that one day might drift in from the sea to her shore and be discovered and read and understood, and forgiven.

ACKNOWLEDGEMENTS

Thank you first to my daughter, for allowing this part of a much bigger story to be told in the hope that it may help someone, somewhere, whether they be mother or daughter.

Thank you to all the writers, poets and musicians, known and unknown, dead and alive, who have guided my way. They have been like stepping-stones across a great chasm of darkness.

I would like to thank Hazel Marshall, my editor, for weaving an invisible thread through the fabric of The Dark Moon. Such a gentle touch; often I could not tell she had been there at all, and yet somehow my words flowed more freely, enhanced by her interventions.

A thousand thank you's to my husband and fellow traveller on this journey, for his warmth and quiet wisdom and his unwavering love for my daughter and myself.

Thank you to my special friends (you know who you are) for helping me get through.

And to Ian Thorp for believing The Dark Moon worthy of publication.

And, last but not least, thank you to those who felt like enemies at the time, those who seemed to go out of their way to make this journey harder and the agony of it more prolonged. For, like the dark characters in every story, they brought us face to face with our own greatest fears; and yet, in so doing, they ultimately led us to the bounty of our own souls, from whose deep terrain we discovered eventually new, organic and previously obscured ways of going forward in the precious relationship with our daughter and in our own evolving lives.

FOREWORD

'The Truth Will Set You Free'. [John 8:31-32]

The impetus behind Desmond Tutu's Truth and
Reconciliation Commission, the knowledge that we can best or
only be healed of trauma and abuse by listening to the stories
of, understanding and ultimately forgiving the perpetrators of
that abuse is the core thread of this powerful book.

The day that Anne Maria and her husband discover that
their teenage daughter has been sexually abused; that their
best friends have supported the girl in her grief and distress;
that all of them have adhered to the vow of silence she has
implored of and imposed on them for at least a year and a half;
that they have unwittingly been living a life of secrets and lies
for all that time, is the day their world falls apart.

For an instant in that moment of awakening to the truth,
Anne Maria feels the presence of angels, and, fleetingly, an
immense empathy with everyone involved. She knows she is
being given a choice. For no reason that is apparent to her,
simply, perhaps, as a gut reaction, she chooses to take what
she calls 'the hard path'. With that, she feels the angel leaving
her and embarks on the longest and most painful journey of
their lives.

And what a hard path it is. Feeling the burden of the
responsibility of the parent to nurture and protect her
daughter, she feels utterly betrayed and is enraged by what her
friends have done as they colluded with her daughter in the
keeping of this huge and traumatic secret, and in entering into
the inevitable web of lies that supported that. Her instinctive
initial reaction is to express her very understandable anger,
which exacerbates the isolation of her and her husband in their

joint misery. The more she rages the more she is abandoned by the very people who could and should have supported her and, inevitably, the more she becomes estranged from herself.

This book and its story detail her long journey to understanding, forgiveness and healing. Every reader will recognise and feel the power of that journey. It is the archetypal journey of all women: Demeter's journey; the loss of the child, their daughter; the wild search for meaning; the plunge into despair and the dark world of the psyche; the overwhelming trials along the way in the seemingly endless search to find a way of reconciling herself with the truths she has discovered, with her daughter, who has locked herself away from her parents, with uncovering the darker aspects of her self and, ultimately, to becoming whole again.

Anne Maria uses poetry, fairy story and myth to support this intimate and brutally honest recording of her initial feelings of helplessness, remorse, and guilt, and to sustain and nurture her epic tale of progress towards her own soul healing in this extraordinarily honest, powerful and beautiful piece of writing. The multiple layers in which she intricately entwines and wraps her story, the way in which she connects and reconnects, weaves these into her emotional progress on the journey, the honesty and lucidity of the expression of her thinking and feeling are emotionally taxing but essential reading for those of us who know that we need to embark – or are already on – our own personal journey toward truth and reconciliation.

Sarah Frossell
October 2008
Cheltenham England
International Coach and Trainer – NLP

PERMISSIONS

The author and publisher gratefully acknowledge the following sources for permission to use copyright material:

Aurora Press, for excerpts from *The Lunation Cycle: Key to the Understanding of Personality*, by Dane Rudhayar.

Darton, Longman & Todd, for excerpts from *Learning to Dance*, by Michael Mayne.

Faber and Faber, for excerpts from *The Wasteland and Other Poems*, and *Four Quartets*, by T. S. Eliot.

HarperCollins, for excerpts from *A Dictionary of Symbols*, by Tom Chetwynd.

Caitlin Matthews, for excerpts from *Sophia: Goddess of Wisdom*.

John Matthews, for excerpts from *The Elements of the Grail Tradition*, and *The Grail Seekers' Companion*, by John Matthews & Marian Green.

Penguin Group, for excerpts from *Myth of the Goddess: Evolution of an Image*, by Anne Baring & Jules Cashford.

The Random House Group, for excerpts from *Women who Run with the Wolves*, by Clarissa Pincola Estes PhD.

Taylor & Francis (Publisher), for excerpts from *The Adolescent Psyche: Jungian and Winnicottian Perspectives*, by Richard Frankel.

The Thorson Publishing Group, for excerpts from *First Steps in Ritual: Magical Techniques for Experiencing the Inner Worlds*, by Dolores Ashcroft-Nowiki.

Visva-Bharati, excerpts from *Gitanjali*, by Rabindranath Tagore.

The Women's Press, for excerpts from *The Moon and the Virgin: Reflections on the Archetypal Feminine*, by Nor Hall.

Wordsworth Editions Ltd., for excerpts from 'The Song of a Man Who Came Through', by D. H. Lawrence, in *The Complete Poems of D. H. Lawrence*.

'Thank You For Hearing Me' Words and Music by Sinead O'Connor and John Reynolds © 1994, Reproduced by permission of EMI Music Publishing Ltd, London WC2H 0QY. At the time of going to press, despite every effort, permission has not been gained from John Reynolds.

CONTENTS

The Dark Moon
The Secret
Paradise Lost
The Wasteland

The Crescent Moon
Sorrowful Wanderings

The Waxing Quarter Moon
Flaming Torches

The Gibbous Moon
The Dark Moon
Lifting the Spell

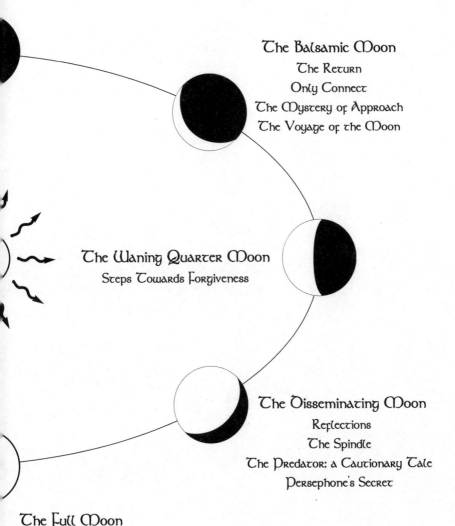

The Balsamic Moon
The Return
Only Connect
The Mystery of Approach
The Voyage of the Moon

The Waning Quarter Moon
Steps Towards Forgiveness

The Disseminating Moon
Reflections
The Spindle
The Predator: a Cautionary Tale
Persephone's Secret

The Full Moon
Calling the Soul Home
The Centre of the Dance

the dark moon

the secret

paradise lost

the wasteland

The Secret

Tears of Isis

Return, oh return!
Oh lovely helper return!
Those that were enemies are no more here.
Return, oh return!
Oh lovely helper return,
That thou mayest see me, thy sister,
Who loves thee,
And comest thou not near me?
Oh beautiful one, return, oh return.
When I see thee not,
My heart sorrows for thee.
My eyes ever seek thee,
I roam about for thee, to see thee
in the form of the Nile,
To see thee, to see thee, thou beautiful loved one.[1]

---

1 Emil Nauman 1882, p. 40

Right now, writing is keeping me alive. It's containing the excesses of my pain, and still it spills over.

Sometimes we write in order to survive. We pour forth our agony onto endless tear-stained pages. We purge ourselves to the dregs and, in so doing, attempt to understand and make sense of our distress. Such understanding, we are counselled, is a pre-requisite of healing, for through it the black-red blood that gushes from our wounds can gradually be abated. But first, we have to face and fully feel our pain.

A Queen's Lament

Alas! that day of mine, on which I was destroyed.
Alas! that day of mine, on which I was destroyed.

For on it he came hither to me in my house,
For on it the boat came on my river toward me,
For on it the boat moored at my quay,
For on it the master of the boat came in toward me,
For on it he reached out his dirty hands toward me,
For on it he yelled to me: 'Get up! Get on board'
For on it my goods were taken aboard in the bow,
For on it I, the queen, was taken on board in the stern.
For on it I grew cold with the most shivering fear.
That foe trampled with his booted feet into my chamber!

That foe reached out his dirty hands toward me!
He reached out his hand toward me. He terrified me!
That foe reached out his hand toward me,
Made me die with fear. [2]

---

2   From an ancient Mesopotamian text. Baring and Cashford 1991, p. 173

Some say that the universe never gives you more than you can handle. I've always agreed and until now I've handled whatever came my way; not brilliantly, necessarily, but I have survived.

It's now nearly six months since 'the secret' was revealed.

It seems uncanny that last year, when my eldest daughter was living in Europe, I became pre-occupied with the symbolism of masks. My husband and I went to a February carnival in full seventeenth-century costume, made a short film of the event and later that year helped to organise a wonderful masked ball for two thousand graduating students back home.

Our youngest daughter, then aged fifteen, was still at school. She had discovered a passion for dancing and was attending lessons with a view to pursuing dance as a career. As far as we could see she was a normal, healthy teenager. There was a deep sense of satisfaction and contentment; all was well in our world.

Then came the series of near-fatal blows that changed our lives beyond recognition. It was as if a million masks all at once tumbled to the ground. Nothing was as we believed it to be. The truth had been hidden. It turned out that many of the people close to us had been keeping a secret – wearing masks, if you like – pretending for a thousand different reasons that our world was okay. It wasn't.

It was more than I could handle. I did not know if I would survive.

Paradise Lost

I am the mother of a sexually abused child.

No! Not me! Not my baby!
Please God, don't let it be true!

But it is true. It has been true for a very long time, though I did not know it to be so. I have been unaware of the secrets and lies that surrounded me, locking me into what feels like the cruellest of illusions about the harrowing reality of what was really going on with my child.

I want to cry out, so loud that all the walls around me shudder and shake and all the windowpanes crack and shatter. I want to scream dementedly: that my child has been abused; that a terrible crime has been committed against her; that she was stolen away into the darkness and could no longer feel my love.

The Wasteland

We have lost the past, the present is bleak,
we are in a wasteland.[3]

As a close friend said: This is where all longing starts.
This is where the great internal journey begins. We make
literal journeys, physical journeys; but we make internal
journeys as well and the two are often very closely related
to one another. And the great internal journey is the search
for paradise lost.[4] This is a universal theme pre-figured in
myth and spiritual teaching across space and time.

When the creation was new and all the stars shone in
their first splendour, the gods held their assembly in the
sky and sang, 'Oh, the picture of perfection!
The joy unalloyed!'

But one cried of a sudden, 'It seems that somewhere
there is a break in the chain of light and one of the
stars has been lost.'

Then the golden string of the harp snapped, the song
stopped, and they cried in dismay, 'Yes, that lost star
was the best, she was the glory of all heavens.'

3   David Patterson, from introduction to *The Quest for the Holy Grail* concert,
     Loughborough University, 1994
4   ibid

From that day the search is unceasing for her, and the
cry goes on from one to the other that in her the world
has lost its joy. [5]

Paradise, of course, is a relative and not an absolute idea.
I am not saying that our life before was perfect. It
wasn't, nor could it be, absolutely. But it was quite all right;
up and down maybe, but in relation to where we are now,
the downs were relatively minor and the ups infinitely
higher. Without a doubt, the revelations of the past year
have precipitated the most profound spiritual crisis. Like
countless story-travellers before us – our prototypes – we
too are in a wasteland, lost, dazed and clueless as to how
and why we have arrived here.

What are the roots that clutch?
What branches grow out of this stony rubbish?
Son of man you cannot say or know,
For you know only a heap of broken images. [6]

Psychologically, we are told that the motif of *brutal loss*
in life, as well as in myth and fairytale, *communicates an*
imperative psychic truth. Unless we pay attention, we are
counselled, unless we heed the warning, wake up, then that
which sustains us spiritually and emotionally, that which
brings joy and meaning to our lives, may be forever *pried*
upon, threatened, robbed or seduced away.... [7]

We need to look at and read 'the writing on the wall'
with as much consciousness as we can muster. We must
summon both courage and humility to revisit our past, to
review the twists and turns we made along the way, see
what signals and messages we unwittingly gave to others,
what signs and clues we missed. We need to ask some tough

5   Gitanjali, in Rabindranath Tagore 1912, p. 72
6   T. S. Eliot, 1940, p. 23
7   C. P. Estes, 1992, p. 218

questions, of ourselves as well as of other people. We must take up the challenge that this tragedy has provided. For ultimately – and this is a core belief of mine – it offers us a chance to transform, if not to undo; a chance to make good. Where hitherto there was weakness, blindness, naïvety, call it what you will, may there be strength, insight, wisdom; love.

What we lose and rediscover in this spirit shall never again be stolen from our hearts.

What we call the beginning is often the end.
And to make an end is to make a beginning.
The end is where we start from.

We shall not cease from exploration,
And the end of all our exploring,
Will be to arrive where we started
And know the place for the first time. [8]

In what follows, our journey is into the past and to the present and to the future. The search is always perilous; the journey is each person's need. The finding of the truth is healing.

I want to be clear at the start that I am not attempting to tell my daughter's story, for much of it remains a closely guarded secret. This is the story of how we as parents experienced and tried to come to terms with the devastating reality we had discovered. My wish is that it will prove to be a story with a happy ending, the story of a journey that leads back to peace and forgiveness for all concerned. It is this wish, this imperative, that draws me to explore the deep shadow that fell across all our lives.

8   T. S. Eliot, 1944, line 240 ff

On the night when the secret was revealed, my daughter stayed away with friends. She didn't come home for several days. When she did she was a stranger.

In the aftermath, I dreamed of endlessly searching, but I could not find her. I awoke sobbing and exhausted. The dreams, whatever else they may have been, revealed a more shocking and personally devastating reality than I could ever have anticipated. My child did not want to be found.

Part of her did, I'm sure, and this was the part towards which I made haste, heart wide open, arms outstretched: 'I am here.' But instead of melting into my embrace, as I had imagined, she recoiled, withdrew and shut me out. Nothing in this world could have prepared me for this. I did not know then what I know now: that parents are often the last people their children can speak to.

Yet it is instinctual for a mother to 'be there' for her children; at least, that was how it felt. How pitifully disorienting to be led away from the hurting instead of towards it. I couldn't comprehend it. This was not how it was meant to be. I was her mother, she my cherished child! I was devastated, totally confused and insanely jealous of all those who continued to support her.

We stumbled through the following weeks and months in a kind of punch-drunken stupor. What should never have happened had happened.

Our world collapsed. We had seriously lost the plot, the track, the scent, call it what you will, and we were reeling. Six months earlier my husband had been made redundant. It had felt *then* as if the rug had been ripped from under our feet. Now the floor had caved in too. There was nowhere to stand.

In order to get any kind of foothold we simply had to track back. We had to come to some kind of understanding of how and for what reason our child had become a stranger overnight. For the next few months I ran round my world like a woman possessed, desperately trying to fill in the missing parts of our lives. The gap was deep and wide, like Tolkien's 'crack of doom'; an underworld issuing forth a dark tale which had been written, all unawares, between the lines of our life – our shadow, if you like – a thundercloud, brim full and fit to burst with years of hidden pain.

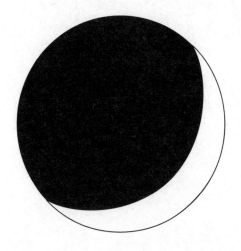

the crescent moon

sorrowful wanderings

Sorrowful Wanderings

*The myth of loss; searching and finding is a lunar myth.
And the search for the lost loved one follows the
course of the moon.* [9]

There are three days of darkness in every lunar cycle
when the moon cannot be seen at all. Symbolically this is
the period when it seems as if 'the beloved' has gone away
for ever and we do not know if she or he will ever come
back. The ancients called it 'the land of no return', for it is
experienced as a complete cessation of the life-process.
Many, many tears are shed during this time; they are called
the Tears of Isis.

At such times, we, like the ancients before us, have only
our faith to sustain us. Yet we are promised that the
darkness is itself transformative, for it is within this
hidden realm, this dark phase of the moon, this deep underworld which is both tomb and womb, that the process of
regeneration mysteriously takes place; and through it the
shape of the future is established and given new form.

The peoples of antiquity took their orientation from the

9   Baring and Cashford, ibid. p. 173

moon, and the mysteries of loss and search were re-enacted in
their temples. Veiled in alternating black and white robes,
the priestesses of old retold the endless story of the loss of
the beloved, of the long search for recovery and of the new
life that issued forth as a result of their quest.

The myth of Demeter and Persephone elucidates this
universal theme. It tells the story of the abduction into the
underworld of a beautiful maiden and the sorrowful
wanderings of her mother as she searches for her lost child.
The grief of Demeter is renowned throughout the classical
world; her pitiful cries of lament echo those of countless
grieving goddesses whose tales of loss and search came to
populate mythology from the third millennium BC.

The grief of Isis knew no bounds and her tears filled the
River Nile. It was the same with the goddess Inanna, and
Ishtar before her; the same in the grief of our own Blessed
Virgin for her crucified son. Here is a hymn for Demeter,
when she lost Persephone:

*Demeter was far away on Mount Olympus when it
happened. When she discovered that her beautiful
child had been stolen, a sharp pain seized her heart.
She tore the veil from her hair, let fall her cloak and
like a solitary wild bird she streaked out across dry
land and sea, searching.*

*Everywhere she asked after the whereabouts of her
child, but no one wanted to tell her the truth, neither
the gods nor mortal men. Not even one true messenger
of the birds of omen came back to her. Eventually the
tender-hearted Hecate, who had heard Persephone's
screams, took pity on Demeter and took her to the son
of Hyperion who knew what had happened.*

'The girl I bore,' wept Demeter,
'That sweet young shoot, lovely to look upon.
I heard her sobbing in the empty air
As if she were being forced against her will,
Though with my eyes I saw nothing.
But you with your rays, you look down from the
                                   luminous air
On all the earth and all the sea.
Tell me your infallible truth about my dear child;
If you saw her anywhere, who was it, far away from me,
Who seized her violently against her will and was gone?
Who of the gods or mortal men?'

So she spoke. And the son of Hyperion answered her.
'Queen Demeter, daughter of the thick-haired Rhea,
You shall know. For greatly do I respect and pity you,
Grieving for your daughter with the slender feet.
There is no other god to blame but Zeus
Who gathers the clouds. He gave her to Hades.'

Pain sharper still and yet more savage came into her heart.
Outraged and shrouded in dark clouds,
she withdrew from the company of gods; from high
Olympus she went down to the cities of men and their
rich fields, disguising her form for a long time.
And no one who saw her knew her,
no man or deep-breasted woman,
until she came to the house of Celeus, lord of
                                   fragrant Eleusis.
Saddened in her heart she sank down near the wayside
of the Maiden Well, where the citizens came to draw water.
She sat in the shade, and branches of an olive tree
grew overhead. And she was like an old, old woman,
Full of her years.... [10]

---

10   Baring and Cashford, ibid. pp. 370-372. From an ancient Greek text.

We were like Demeter: no one had been able to tell us the truth. Even after we knew, some of those people who had known what happened turned us away.

It was eerie visiting those who agreed to see me. At first I clutched onto the vain hope that they wouldn't know why I was knocking on their doors. But they all did. Confirmation, stark and unequivocal. It was all I could do to keep standing; not to faint, not to collapse there and then on their doorsteps.

I can't tell you how disorienting it is to discover that your world is not as you believed it to be. Looking back at that time, remembering, it was as if I'd been hit round the head with a cricket bat. At times I felt like one of those pathetically wounded cartoon characters that stumble across the screen with a circle of stars depicting dizziness and disorientation buzzing around them. It's easy to lose your footing in such circumstances. You don't know who you are any more, nor how the people around you relate to your own life. As with Alice through the Looking Glass, everything's upside down and back to front and inside out and you cannot get your bearings.

Most people took me in, gave me tea or sharp shots of brandy and told me what they knew. Some just held me whilst I wept. The majority understood the absolute psychological necessity for us to fill in the gaps, to get a grip on what had happened. A whole year, if not more, was missing from our lives. They could see us floundering badly. It had all come so suddenly. The need to track back, to piece it all together, felt like a matter of life and death.

We needed to talk, over and over again, just to preserve our sanity. Those who understood and accommodated us provided a lifeline, dredging us up from the deep chaos into which we had fallen and in which we were in grave danger of drowning. It was difficult for all concerned and, tragically, several long-standing and important relationships were severed at this point. After a while the people concerned refused to speak to us altogether, and some acted to prevent us having contact with yet others who had kept the secret.

Why was the subject closed? Why couldn't we hear what they had to say? I could not comprehend it. These people were our only source of information; talking to them felt like the only possible way of threading the shreds of our torn reality back together, for the fragments of the story we were gathering didn't add up. There were anomalies that greatly exacerbated our distress. Some said that there had been just one incident of abuse; others relayed a yet more harrowing tale.

In my desperation I pleaded, demanded, threatened. After all, it was my right; or, at least, this was how it felt. Our child was under age; we were her parents; surely friends and family would understand our need to know, to be included, make sense, stop ourselves going crazy? I drove myself half to madness in the pursuit of these things. Mostly, it came to nothing.

You see, it was the loss of relationship with our child that we couldn't understand, much less cope with. We quickly discovered that her reactions fitted a very common category of response, but living with it proved more than we could bear. We blamed ourselves, felt sure that on some level we had failed as parents.

Once upon a time we had been so close.

There are oceans of tears women have never cried....
But in truth, for the sake of a woman's wild soul, it is
better to cry. [11]

I wept every single day for ten months, sometimes wildly,
out of control, sometimes silently, brokenly, wanting to die.

My daughter wept too, alone and with her *confidantes*
but not with me. Behind the scenes, behind the curtains that
had been drawn so tightly shut across the trauma, she had
been living a nightmare. 'She told me on your birthday last
year,' one of my best friends explained after the secret came
out. 'Sometimes she would just call and sob for hours.
Other times she would ask me to drive over and get her
because she just couldn't cope at all.' When I challenged
my friend about why she had not told me, she replied, 'She
just couldn't bear for you to know.'

It is almost impossible to believe that I did not pick up
on my daughter's torment. But I did not: she kept it so tight,
and those in whom she did confide were sworn to
secrecy. So the year had proceeded in a haze of illusion.
Nearly twenty people, most importantly she herself, were
caught in an impossible moral dilemma, until eventually
someone, like Hecate in the Demeter and Persephone myth,
'heard her screams' and came forward, saying that her life
was spinning out of control as a result of what had happened.
That was when she gave permission for us to be told, albeit
in scant detail.

Like most mothers of young teenagers, I thought I knew
where she was at all times. I was wrong; so wrong. More
than anything I wanted to slap myself awake, not in a
sadistic way, but more like a Zen master who cracks his
stick over the shoulder of a novice monk losing

---

11   Estes, ibid. p. 374

concentration during meditation practice. You see, looking back I can see how unconscious I have been. There is something about trust that is so strong, so incredibly hard to break. I believed my world as it was presented to me. Most people do. I thought my relationships with my friends and with my daughter were straightforward. I was wrong.

Where there are secrets, there are lies. Where there are lies, more lies are required to protect them. The situation quickly goes out of control, relationships change, and no one really understands why. Something is sensed; sniffed, so to speak. Reassurances are given, but we are not completely reassured.

There is no way in this world that we could have imagined what was really going on. However, I had known that my relationship with my daughter was changing. I'd put it down to adolescence. It was reasonable to do so. I had accepted the fact that she was not as open as I would have expected her to be. I was sorry, but did not intrude beyond her boundaries. I missed her painfully, but accepted the fact that she was growing up. We missed our friends too, many of whom seemed to be giving us a wide berth. We reasoned it was because my husband had recently had to leave his job. It wasn't; yet how could we possibly have known otherwise?

What lay before us at that time was an unimaginably harrowing journey. The next few months were the most gruelling I have ever experienced. At the end of the summer my husband said he had 'lost his soul.' In time, we would discover a route that led out of this hell, a route that led, not directly back home, but at least to a place where we could breathe. First, however, we had to confront our rage.

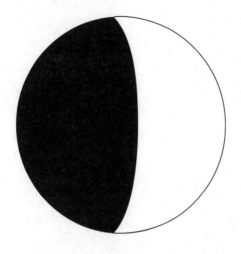

the waxing quarter moon

flaming torches

Flaming Torches

Underneath rage is this:

> *Something has happened to hope. Behind the loss of*
> *hope is usually anger; behind anger, pain; behind*
> *pain, torture of one sort or another, sometimes recent,*
> *but often from long ago.* [12]

There was a moment, brief though it was, that occurred
the instant I was told the news; just before I sank to my
knees in gut-staggering shock and my world changed
beyond recognition. There was a moment. And in it an
angel seemed fleetingly close by, a wise presence of some
kind. And it seemed I was offered a choice: an easy way or
a hard one. Without intending I chose the hard way, and the
angel promptly left my side.

But in that moment, I saw it all as if through 'angels'
eyes'. Maybe it was the rush of adrenaline and all the shock
mechanisms that somehow blasted me out of my body and
into some other realm where angels seem quite common-
place. And from there I felt utter compassion for everyone
who had kept me from the truth, and my heart went out to
them, each and every one, and I was grateful for the help

---

12   Estes, ibid. p. 352

they had given my child. Though as the seconds passed, the agony of the crime and of the betrayal seized me and I crashed into despair.

As a consequence, part of me lived the next few years in torment. For what I craved most – to stand together, to hold hands against the darkness – was refused and no matter how hard I clamoured to be let back into the fold, the doors of those I loved and trusted were locked even tighter against me.

But suddenly, after a long time, some said there could be a possibility of compromise, that I could return. My heart leapt, but plummeted within seconds. I must not speak of what had gone on between us. It was the thing I found impossible to accept. For without acknowledgement, without understanding and confrontation of the problem, it seemed to me that the prohibited life would always be between us, like a ghost, a trapped and unquiet thing, neither fully dead nor fully free to depart. And no matter what, it would be there, obstructing intimacy, congruency, healing.

'I'm not dead!' it would cry out, its anguish splintering into the desolate spaces between us. 'I'm not dead!' But it would be a silent cry, that only those of us concerned would hear. And my fear was that if I agreed to keep silent, this cry would get louder and louder and more insistent, despite our best intentions, until in the end we wouldn't be able to hear ourselves over and above its din. And maybe then we would start to say that we didn't much enjoy each other's company and maybe then we would drift apart for good, because when we were together, we would be haunted.

But, even worse than this, I feared relationships where even the troubled ghosts had ceased to cry out and there would be nothing to remind us. And even if we agreed between ourselves that the ghost was finally dead, that we were free, slowly, imperceptibly, a numbness would creep over us and we would wonder less and less how we came to be this way. Yet by then we would have forgotten anyway, even if we could remember to ask the question; and either way, we would still be haunted.

We must do what we can to lay our ghosts to rest. Then we may live properly again. I still believe this, even though I have seen how utterly unattainable it can seem. Looking back, it was then that I seemed to become like the ghost myself; I haunted my world, wailing into the ever increasing silence around me. And sure enough, it happened that all those I haunted wanted to see me even less, and as time passed I found myself more and more hosting not only the disquiet in my own soul but that of the entire situation, and my world filled up with the din of what was not given a voice elsewhere.

When Demeter first discovered that Persephone had been stolen, she went crazy. Inconsolable in her grief, she also gave vent to a wild, primordial rage. She flew down from Mount Olympus in a fury, flaming torches clasped in her hands, bellowing to the gods to set her daughter free.

She raged, she wept, she screamed, she searched every land formation underneath, inside and atop, begged mercy, begged death; but no matter what, she could not find her heart-child. [13]

For, as we have seen, gods and mortals alike ignored her, clinging to the belief that eventually she would come to terms with her loss. But the more she was refused, the more her rage was inflamed until eventually, in one final and

---

13   Estes, ibid. p. 338

terrible act of defiance, she brought the cycle of the seasons to an end and refused to allow time to turn until her beautiful daughter was returned to her side.

From that day forward a dark winter came over the earth and Demeter, like Persephone, sank down into its depths. Nothing could grow thereafter. No one could live as before; but neither could they die nor yet be born, for the goddess withheld even the seeds of creation from humanity, so angry and defiant was her heart.

This is the power of the archetypal feminine as expressed in the image of the wrathful goddess: pure, instinctual, raw and completely unrestrained by the brake of consciousness that functions to temper and civilise our responses to crimes committed against our children. Yet beyond the parameters of acceptable and civilised expressions of emotion, all parents of abused children, and all who reel in the tragic estrangements that routinely follow in the wake of such crimes, must contend with grief and with rage no less powerful than that of Demeter for her stolen child.

If only we too could stop time. If only! If only!

Rape and sexual abuse are endemic in our culture. At the time of writing, one in six children will be abused in this way before the age of sixteen. At root, such crimes are about the abuse of power, power over other human beings. Boys, girls, men and women have been victims for centuries, but it is an inescapable fact that the vast majority are female, like the ancient Queen and her daughters whose harrowing lament we quoted at the start.

Her words contain all this history, all this deep-rooted

collective memory, and all this found a place of resonance within me. It hacked into an ancient wound in my soul, something that had lain low for a long time. Now it was ripped open again; but this time it was not only the ancient queen and her daughters, not only Persephone and all the countless generations of women and girls, including me, subjected to the abuse of power down the ages. Now it was my daughter too.

Such crimes are a feature of patriarchal culture, in which women and girls have frequently been objectified, devalued, disrespected and unlawfully possessed. It's everybody's business, for every time something like this happens it happens to all of us, to all our daughters. Our pain is collective and personal, all at the same time.

Somehow we think we are going to be able to protect our children from the wickedness of the world. I know it seems naïve but, really, this is how millions of mothers begin. Our stories are brand new, you see, at the beginning. Or so it seems. And even though we know of the dark side of life, that everywhere under the sun there is also evil, we believe that we can steer a different course. Mothers almost of necessity must begin in this way, with a kind of blind faith, with hope.

For fourteen years everything had gone well for us in this respect. We had loved, protected and nurtured our child, or so we believed. The shock of realising that a crime had been committed against her without our knowledge was completely debilitating, for it shattered the illusion of safe passage that we had nurtured since her birth. As a result we just fell apart.

This of course is where all sacred journeys begin.

Inevitably, rage is part of this story, part of Demeter's story. It's a difficult part, an unruly part, a 'smeltering' volcanic mass which, pushed repeatedly back, only becomes more urgent for release. Like most people, I would rather it didn't show up. I would rather not deal with it. But it came anyway; it had to, like the Thirteenth Fairy at the Sleeping Beauty's christening party. She hadn't been invited, you see, even though her gifts were potentially as enriching as those of her sisters.

What she really wanted was to be included.

Instead, she ended up as one of the most despised figures of fairytale. There are shades of Demeter in the Thirteenth Fairy and shades of both in my reactions towards those who shut me out. I can't deny these things. But, like Sleeping Beauty's mother, I also have been the victim of a dark enchantment. Of course we don't realise that we have been given a magical sleeping potion by those in whom we placed our trust, until we wake up to it. Then: anger, indignation, defiance; rage.

To be betrayed by our culture; by an unknown man, a damaged, predatory soul who would probably never know the meaning of respect, of honour, of right action; this was one thing. It haunted me. I couldn't get it out of my mind. But on top of this, to have been blindfolded and ushered into the mists of a false reality by our own family and friends, to be turned away, even now, by those I had trusted most, just about finished me off.

Was this not also my world, my story, my family, my child? Didn't it reach down into the depths of the earth and struggle back upward through the soil, pushing, stretching, clutching toward the light? Shouldn't the cry have gone out amongst us all that a predator was at work in our midst?

For if not our friends and family, if not the ones we trust, then who will tell us when our enemy is approaching, who will warn us of his dark intention? And who will protect our children when he strikes in the night?

Where was the solidarity in all this?

To be 'protected' from such a truth felt like the most brutal betrayal, the deadliest of cards a mother can be dealt, her worst nightmare; for it severs the connection, hacks asunder the invisible umbilical chord through which she nurtures and protects her child. It cuts her off from the child whom she loves at the very moment when in her heart she believes that she is needed most.

The cruel irony in our story is that our daughter was desperately trying to protect us from the pain of it all. But it went tragically wrong for all concerned.

So if, as a reader, you bleed for our loss, you are right to do so, for there is nothing in this world, no pain, no river of unimaginable sorrow, greater than that of a parent for her wounded child or of a daughter for her parents' pain. For, you see, the trap, the exile, works both ways.

The consequences are profound, as both history and mythology bear witness. Spiritually we are cast into the wilderness, where we must wander for forty days and forty nights, or one hundred years, or many lives, struggling to get back to where we began. We are keening; reeling. The shock of separation is more than we can bear.

What I wished more than anything is that someone could have foreseen the damage that this dual exile would inflict upon us all and acted to prevent it. They didn't have to break my daughter's confidence; a clue that she was in trouble might have been all we needed to steer a different course. As it turned out, we were driven into hell.

So let me give it to you straight!

I am broken.

I am on my knees in grief at the abuse of my child.

But I'm also livid with those who deceived me.

If they were going to take it upon themselves to deprive myself and my husband of our parental responsibility – our ability to respond – if they saw fit, for whatever reason, to appropriate that role, then they should also have taken up the massive responsibility that goes with it.

A huge part of being a parent is about protecting one's children. It's an awesome responsibility. And I have to say to those who deceived us, thus making it impossible for us to protect our child: why the hell didn't they do the job properly?

Let me spell it out.

First, I wonder if any of them had made themselves conversant with the basic literature on child sexual abuse? I don't think so, for if they had they would have understood instantly that they needed to protect our child from further attack. The day after I heard I spoke to a friend who works as a psychotherapist with sexually-abused young adults.

'She must never return to the place where it happened and must never, ever, be left alone with him again, because once such a boundary is broken, it is broken irretrievably and the risk of further abuse is greatly increased.'

It took me less than twelve hours to accrue this vital information, and much besides. You can imagine how crazy I felt, knowing that since the assault my child had indeed returned to the home of the abuser. Who was looking out for her then?

Second, they needed to make sure that she was checked for sexually-transmitted diseases. As it turns out her attacker was sexually promiscuous. Did they even think about this? Some diseases can result in infertility if not treated within the first twelve months.

Third, in entering a pact of secrecy with our child they went against the advice of all the major helping agencies. It is for good reason that the NSPCC use the slogan, *Don't Keep It to Yourself*. If you phone any of the National help-line numbers as I did, they will tell you that the advice they give to abused children who phone in is this:

Find a trusted adult and tell them as quickly as possible.

It is hoped that the designated adult will do the right thing and intervene to prevent the possibility of further assault to the child, and also to protect others who may be at risk. As it turned out, several young people were being systematically abused by this man; but whilst ever the crimes against my daughter were kept secret this could not come to light. Because of lack of communication, coupled with the failure to read the signs and make important connections, we all actually ended up facilitating the abuser. Unintentionally of course, but with profound consequences nevertheless.

Fourth, by sanctioning a culture of lies – a secret life, a double life – all healthy channels of communication, possibilities for authenticity, congruency, and basic trust were eroded. By the time I was eventually told, my daughter had been so totally cut off from me, my love, protection, support and compassion, had grown so used to weaving a web of illusion around us, that our relationship had been reduced to a hollow sham in the very places that matter most. By implication, all those who agreed to keep the secret communicated to our daughter that it was not only OK for her, as a fifteen year old, to carry the burden of something so massive, without any reference to her immediate family, but also that this was an acceptable way for her to live, forever staving off the inevitable changes that disclosure would bring.

Sometimes things need to change. To be held in a condition of contrived stasis inhibits the natural process of change and the deep journey of transformation which the crime against her necessitated for all concerned. Moreover, adherence to this 'culture of lies' robbed us as a family of the possibility of a more enlightened approach, the chance to do it differently, to break the mould, change the pattern and do the work we needed to do. Where there are secrets, however, '*the psychological purpose of family – to pull together – never occurs*'. [14]

And what of the consequences for the soul? I wonder how many of the people who kept her confidence were aware of the absolutely deleterious effects on the psyche of

14   Estes, ibid. p. 384

living a lie? Let me enlighten you! The soul cannot live fully in such cramped conditions. It cannot sing out, or dance and play. It cannot look fully into the eyes of its loved ones, for fear of caving in, for fear of being true. And in such cramped, fear-ridden conditions, part of the self withers and sometimes even dies.

What a tragic twist of fate that this same silence is then upheld by those who would support our young people; for very different reasons no doubt – good, sound reasons – but with devastating spin-offs nevertheless. For little by little, everyone involved is thoroughly compromised, whilst the offender is left in the community, free to offend again.

These are massive dilemmas. The case is strong on both sides, as we shall see. Yet in order to proceed, as proceed we must, we have at the very least to acknowledge that there are *two truths* to the matter of secrets: the truth about the need and right to confidentiality, which despite everything we still do uphold; and the truth about what it costs to keep such secrets safe.

Fifth, and related to the above: did anyone consider what this deception would do to us? Let me say, it has completely shattered our trust. If I had known as a girl growing up that one day I would be here, I don't think I could have found the courage to live.

Sixth: everyone in my daughter's support group was placed in a moral dilemma. I see this. *'Torment'* was how one friend described it after I found out and challenged them. *'We talked about it every night, walked up to your house several times but always turned back, went to phone you on numerous occasions, but never completed the call. If*

*she had been any younger I would have told you straight
away; but she was nearly sixteen when she spoke to me.'*

I understand, truly I do; *and* I have to say how crushing
the deceit has been for me personally. The impact: it feels
as if people did not see me for who I can at best be. This hurts
really badly. Why, oh why, did you confine me within such
a narrow definition of motherhood, and assume I might
only exist in relation to my child within the parameters of
some generalised, reductionist stereotype of an interfering
and dis-empowering mother.

Since the secret was disclosed, I have had to endure a
closed and righteous attitude from several people, and have
even been told that I have not in fact been betrayed. The
phone has been slammed down on me several times. People
have taken the moral high ground, asserting my child's
statutory right to secrecy, telling me I couldn't have done
anything anyway, that only a detached professional can or
could help; effectively, that there was and is no role for me
whatsoever.

I vehemently refute this.

It can't have been easy to speak to me after the secret
came out, but those who agreed to talk have very possibly
saved my life. They have allowed my outrage and also my
compassion for their personal predicaments. More
importantly they have allowed me to discover something of
what my daughter experienced during that terrible period of
her life and to begin to fathom the reasoning behind her
disappearance from my world.

It takes courage to face, to feel the consequences of our
actions, to examine our own part in the tragedy, the

meltdown of an entire family. I know, for I have to face it too. But to wash our hands like Pontius Pilate does not in the end absolve us from the consequences of our choices.

For one thing, if these people thought they would not meet my wrath, they were wrong. If they thought I was 'too nice' to spit venom, they didn't really know me. And maybe I didn't really know that part of myself. There is a time for rage; a time when it is not only justified but required. This is surely one of those times; maybe even the only time in my life when I need to tip back my head, as Clarissa Pincola Estes prescribes, and howl with all my might!

Can anyone stand it? Some can. Some have. Some can't. Others won't. This latter group, on meeting my anger, advised me to go to the doctor instead. They said I was having a nervous breakdown. But hang on a minute! Who was really behaving unreasonably here? Those who went behind my back, those who would not allow me to speak to others who might help me understand, because I'd ranted and raved and might rant and rave again at them? Come on! What sort of a mother would I be if I'd just said, '*Oh! Ok! My daughter's been raped. Maybe more than once. Maybe others are at risk. But I see you've got it in hand. So I'll just get on with my life and pretend that nothing's happened! Maybe one day, in years to come when I've calmed down, as you say, you might fill me in with the details. But no rush! In your own time!*'

Now, I ask you: does that seem very motherly to you? Look, I did not begin in rage. I first arrived broken and grief-stricken at your doors. Rage came afterwards, when those same doors slammed shut in my face.

Anger, you see – and this cuts both ways – is partly the result of not feeling heard, being misunderstood, being pushed into a corner from which instinctively we must fight to be free. Those who blank us unfailingly find themselves on the wrong side of this anger, because the blanking is experienced as hugely provocative. Why? Because it leaves us exactly where we don't want to be: isolated, disempowered, trapped. It is then that we reach for our 'Flaming Torches'; then that our anger, thus prodded and provoked, finally mutates into a thunderous rage. It is then that we become wild, that we erupt like bats out of hell, like Demeter, like the thirteenth fairy, like me; like maybe even you.

And those who blank us become the very people at whom we scream the loudest 'No!' What we are really screaming 'no' to is the collapse of these relationships. We may be in the same room, the same house, the same country, yet we are as far apart as it is possible to be; and it is torture.

But what if we could really understand where the other was coming from? What if we could pull together instead of pulling apart? What if we could each bring something mindful to these terrible times?

In my wishful mind I've often imagined us sitting together at a big table, presided over by some wise old being who is privy to the secrets of all our hearts. And as we listen to each other's stories, understanding dawns, hurt and bitterness dissolves, common ground is recovered, and forgiveness peeps its head over the horizon. Chances are that given the humility to listen and the courage to tell our parts truthfully, something of immense value would emerge, something that would begin to bridge the aching gap that has fallen open between us.

This is what I hoped for at the start and somewhere deep inside I still do hope. I hope for all of us who have lived through these things, for those who are living through them still and for those who will know them in the future. And my hope is this: that in the end we will find a way of standing together, of holding each other's hands, of letting each other back into our deep, deep hearts.

This is what I've really been missing. It's what I've been weeping about, what I've been raging about: this terrible estrangement and loss of one another that has followed in the wake of these crimes. So I pray into this darkness and I send up my prayers to the heavens above, like Isis, who wept for the return of her beloved, at the time of the Dark Moon.

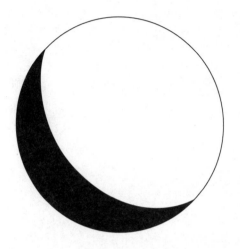

the gibbous moon

the dark moon
lifting the spell

The Dark Moon

Where there is gross injury, the soul flees. [15]

Deep down, many a person knows what it is to be an innocent child, terrorised in a place that they believed was safe. They have once upon a time felt secure, wrapped up, so to speak, in a mother's protective womb. Then, without warning, they have been attacked and mown down. Such atrocities are not easily overcome. They are deep woundings that continue to affect us even when we drive the memory of them into the depths of our unconscious. As a result, our normal development is arrested in ways which can take years to overcome.

When someone leaves, goes away outwardly, it's incredibly hard to bear. When they retreat *inwardly* from even the ones who love them most, the pain of separation is just as intense, from whichever side. Sometimes experiences are too much to bear. To fall out of consciousness would be a merciful release; or at the very least to disassociate ourselves from the distress within. This moment is well documented in myth and fairytale. In the story of the

---

15 Estes, ibid. p. 194

Sleeping Beauty, as we shall see, the retreat is symbolised by a deep, trance-like sleep.

From the heart of the palace, where the beautiful princess had fallen, there rippled throughout a most potent spell of sleep. The king and queen, who had just arrived in the great hall for the birthday celebrations, fell to sleep on their thrones, all the birthday guests who had been arriving fell asleep as they stood, the servants who were busy preparing the birthday feast fell asleep at their work, the king's horses fell asleep in the stables, the dogs in the yard and even the flies on the walls.

Not a living thing remained awake, for all that was mortal slipped into a deep and dreamless river of sleep. And in that same instant, the sun darkened and faded from the skies and a dense forest of cruel thorn encircled the entire palace. For one hundred years, all was lost and hidden from view.

Remember, Remember, Remember.

In the Quest for the Holy Grail, itself a womb-like, moon-like symbol of the feminine realm, the moment of retreat occurs in the immediate aftermath of the terrible rape of the Muses. The Muses kept the Holy Vessel and served its draught of Paradise to all who travelled within the enchanted realms. Afterwards the land was laid waste, the mysterious castle where the Holy Grail was held vanished, and paths to the courts of joy therein were lost beyond recall.

I have been told that during the assault my daughter froze. I am crazy with rage when I think about it. My mind wants to run away, to hide, to think of anything but. It seeps through anyway, every night, as soon as my head hits the pillow, and then I know with every fibre of my being the hell into which she was stolen.

'*When she woke up the morning after,*' a friend of my daughter told me, '*she knew that she was changed forever. She said that she'd gone to bed the night before as an innocent child and woken up as an adult, a different person.*' The happy life she had lived to that point had not protected her. Now she must protect herself. She must harden up, wise up, get real. '*It wasn't so much a decision,*' the friend went on, '*she just woke up like that.*'

Tracking back has been like threading together strands of a coarse, barbed rope with which to lash myself to near oblivion. It's been a long, slow, tortuous revelation, a drip feed, preceded by years of silence; and I still have the sense that I don't know the half of it.

I do know that what happened has completely changed our relationship with our daughter, now a young woman. Nine months after the secret came out, we still had not spoken directly about what happened, had not been allowed to comfort her, cry with her, hold her in our arms, be a mother, father, friend, a sister or brother-in-arms. She was still in retreat, still hidden behind a hedge of thorn, still totally inaccessible to us, her wounds obscured but most probably still raw and in need of tending.

One hundred years is a long time in the passing and many who dwelt within sight of the forest grew old and died pondering its mystery. Yet those who lived at the very edge of the wood had the clearest inklings as to what had happened and, as they sat around their ғιʀᴇs on cold wιnᴛᴇʀ eveninɢs, ᴛhey would weave ᴛhese inklinɢs ᴀnd imᴀɢininɢs inᴛo sᴛʀᴀnɢe ᴀnd mysᴛᴇʀious ᴛᴀles oғ ᴀ бeᴀuᴛiғul pʀincess who lᴀy sleepinɢ wiᴛhin.

Our predicament as parents is pre-figured in this motif: sitting on the edge of the forest, speculating but never really knowing, except in a general sense, what really happened to cause the forest of thorn to rise up and enclose the entire palace. But, like the folk on the very edge of the wood, we too had our inklings. With hindsight we could see that there were signs along the way that something had gone wrong. While we waited for the spell to run its course, we had time to ponder.

We are told that the unconscious leaks its secrets, one way or another. We just can't keep the lid on. The truth will out, maybe in ways we might not expect. Secrets like these are too big to contain, even when it is our conscious intention to do so.

During the making of the Carnival Film I had asked my daughter and her best friend to dress up in masks and carnival costumes. Wanting to create an evocative opening to the film, I had taken them to the grounds of a lovely monastery to film a slow-motion sequence from which I would cut and 'dissolve' into the European city scenes, which were at that time still unfilmed.

We were all a little anxious that day; the light was fading by the time we arrived and the girls were understandably self-conscious, all dressed up as they were. Initially everything went well, but I soon became aware of my daughter's dark mood. When I focused my attention on her friend, encouraging her to perform for the camera, my daughter seemed to become insecure. She appeared angry with me; eventually she refused altogether to participate and ran off through the gardens. I was bewildered. It all came right out of the blue. I ran after her, desperately trying to get my head round what was going on. I found her in a deeply symbolic place.

The enclosed path through the monastery gardens depicts the Stages of the Cross. It is designed as a walking meditation: visitors retrace the steps of Christ on his long walk up to Calvary. At the pinnacle, atop a steep outcrop of rock, a life-size cross is hung with the dying Saviour. Beyond and below, in the distance, lies a replica of the tomb into which his body was placed after his death. It's a little stone building housing a reclining statue of Christ, with his sorrowful mother bent in grief beside him. This is where I found my child, rocking back and forth, tears streaming down her face, her carnival mask discarded on the floor beside her.

I knew in my gut that I could not enter this place, this protective sanctuary into which she had fled. I stood outside, legs like jelly, not knowing what to do. She did not acknowledge my presence. I was still thinking she was jealous of the attention I had shown her friend; but, then, this was far too dramatic a reaction. I remember that the feelings I had at the time were of total non-comprehension of the intensity of her response. It felt extremely dark, out of proportion to my 'offence'.

Part of me was angry with her for pulling out of the session. I had put a lot of energy into the costumes and so on, and she knew how important it was to me. But if the film had been my focus up until that point, it certainly wasn't any more. I was frightened, out of my depth, with no idea what the hell was going on.

The symbolism screamed at me, 'Wake up! Wake up!, But I didn't know what to wake up to. 'Whatever's the matter?' I asked, peering into the tomb from the outside. Blank. Blank. But she looked like thunder. I was only certain that I couldn't go in, couldn't scoop her up in my arms, dry her tears and carry her home. No. The message was absolutely clear: Keep out! Keep out! Private Enclosure!

After a few minutes she got up and rushed past me to the car. Her best friend's mother was driving. The atmosphere in the car was unbearable; to make it even more excruciating for all concerned, our driver had to stop off at a house in a village to pick something up from a colleague. My daughter and I were invited in, given tea and left alone in the sitting room whilst the others sorted out their business. I have never seen my child look so strange; her eyes were quite wild, and blank all at the same time, glazed almost and glaring. Totally confused and unable to compute my reality, I continued to ask her what was wrong.

'Just leave it, Mum,' she said; but it was as if she was speaking from a million miles away.

'But I don't understand.'

She looked me in the eye, but not really. She said, 'I'm going mad!'

All this happened one and a half years before the secret was disclosed.

The following day she seemed completely normal, back to her old familiar self. When I tried to seek clarification about what had happened she dismissed me, saying it was nothing, she'd just got a bit jealous. Months later I edited the footage from that day, slowed it down and added a soundtrack; in the end I used about thirty seconds' worth of images. Looking back, now that the secret's out, is very peculiar. The opening shot is of two masked faces, staring directly into my lens.

Retrospectively of course, the symbolism is easier to interpret. My carnival project had been focused upon what masks could *reveal*, rather than what they might conceal. I see now that the masks in question both revealed and concealed at the same time. Another story was being told that day, as well as the one that I was consciously telling. Stripped to its essentials and with the benefit of hindsight, the symbolism of what was being presented was full of meaning.

A part of my daughter was in retreat, simultaneously concealing and revealing her distress. She was showing me that she needed a safe place with secure boundaries, a sanctuary that could not be violated. In truth, her unconscious spoke: '*Look! This is where I am on the inside. This is what is behind my happy mask: the lies, the painful deception. Some part of me wants you to see, as graphically as I can lay it out. You cannot come in; you may not know why and for what reason; but I want you to look, I want you to see something of my distress.*' It was just a fleeting glimpse behind the scenes, a brief opening, a window into an unknown world where part of her self lived in exile; but it was soon slammed shut by another aspect, the part that emphatically could not bear me to see at all.

Now, in the quest for the Holy Grail, many brave knights set forth into the forest, striking out, one here and one there; and each vowed never to rest until the holy Vessel was recovered and the wasteland healed of its wounds. But of the many who set forth, three alone were destined to succeed. And these included Sir Percival, the Mystic Fool, whose story we shall take up briefly here, for it was to him that a path was eventually revealed to the lost castle where the Grail was hidden.

There he was welcomed by a rich fisherman who led him to a small chapel within, where a wounded king cried out in torment. And there he witnessed a magnificent procession, led by a damsel of pure and matchless beauty, who bore the holy Grail itself, veiled with a cloth of silk.

But, following the advice of his mother, Sir Percival remained politely silent and failed to question the meaning of these things. And straight away, the castle and all its inhabitants vanished and the young knight found himself all alone once more in the pathless wastes of the forest. And there, very soon after, the beautiful damsel who had borne the holy Grail appeared to him, though her countenance and her form were much changed and it seemed to our hero as if all the weight of time had come suddenly upon her.

And, weeping bitterly, she rebukes him for his failure to ask the essential question, which she tells him has much prolonged the agony of the wounded king, who can now neither die nor find relief from his torment. Nor can the wasteland, nor her own lost youth, ever be restored until that question is finally asked.

Well, for seven years thereafter Sir Percival wandered the forest, seeking endlessly to retrace his steps. And during that period, that which was light appeared darkly to him, and that which was dark shed out abundant light. And in this way he was put severely to the test and helped and hindered according to his need.

You see, it's not just a question of seeing, as I discovered to my cost; it is possessing the ability to read the symbolism of what is being presented, and the wisdom to remember the good advice we have been given along the way, and use it, even in the midst of emotionally-fraught circumstances. It's so, so delicate! One wrong move and the whole thing disappears, the doors slam shut, up comes the thorny hedge and, before you know it, it's *one hundred years* of ponderings and imaginings, inklings about what is going on behind. We had no idea of the hidden secret, that day in the monastery gardens; but since its disclosure I have thought of it often and wondered how much suffering could have been avoided if I had had my wits more fully about me.

In myth and fairytale there is always a right way and a wrong way: a right stone to tread upon, one that takes you forward, and one that collapses beneath your feet. The hero: what distinguishes him from his many contemporaries is that when at last he arrives, he understands where, when and exactly how to tread.

Lifting the Spell

The Sleeping Beauty is a typical fairytale.
It starts – once upon a time – with a curse
but ends – happily ever after – with redemption.

Fairytales show us the way out: how to lift the spell that has plunged the palace into darkness and bring about the conditions of release – the reawakening of our souls.

Now, the story of the sleeping princess spread far and wide and many brave knights came and tried to hack their way through the entangled forest in order to settle the matter once and for all. But it was not the destiny of such men to penetrate the wood and despite their fine weapons many got hopelessly caught and trapped within the thicket and were never seen again.

The secrets of the inner world are never revealed to people of such intention. To stand any chance whatsoever the hero must approach in the correct way. The question of *approach* is a key motif in many stories, and the consequences of using any kind of force are spelled out in no uncertain terms. The hero must come to her on precisely the correct day, in the correct season. He must come to her when she wills it; if she is not prepared, if he forces the gates of her sanctuary, if he takes up arms against her, he will not succeed.

In the story of the Sleeping Beauty, this rescuing power is symbolised in the figure of the Prince. He will come at the *right time*, when the hundred years are done; but crucially, according to a twelfth-century Persian version, he will arrive with the accumulated *wisdom* of the sages of the world. It stands to reason then that, if we are ever to glimpse the sleeper behind the hedge of thorn, we too should make ourselves conversant with as much of this wisdom as we can lay our hands on.

Where can such wisdom be found? From the shaman? The storyteller? The tales themselves are surely such a source, as are the words of thinkers of our own time who have studied in depth the theme of adolescence. For the image of the sleeping girl encircled by a hedge of thorn is quintessentially an image of adolescence. The thorny hedge symbolises a necessary defence by which the vulnerable and invariably injured soul seeks to protect itself. Winnicot writes that adolescent defences *offer a protective cocoon, shielding an internal process from impingement by the external world.* [16]

From the outside we might experience the hedge of thorn as being patrolled day and night by an aspect of the self whose sole duty is to protect. If we approach too soon, too late, with the wrong attitude, we are summarily attacked and driven back. Cruel things are said, cutting to the quick, fending off intruders with icy glare and vicious tongue. We

---

16   Winnicott, in Frankl 1998, p. 35

reel. But afterwards such insults must be forgotten and excused, for they are said in passion motivated by dread.

> *Without sensing that the powerful and complicated experiences our adolescents live through are aiming toward something, we unwittingly become over-involved and rob them of their ability to draw upon their own resources for survival during these difficult years. Our natural tendency (as parents and helpers) is to want to step in and take charge.*[17]

Often it is better to practise restraint for, even with the best intentions, our efforts can become counterproductive for ourselves and intrusive for the young person concerned. Frankel is careful to remind us that *the wounding that comes with the shattering of innocence … creates a move toward a more self-protective and enclosed place.*[18]

It is agonising for the parents of adolescents (let alone for the abused adolescents themselves) even to begin to accept this rupture in their relationships with their children. But we should, if we are able, resist the temptation to take it too personally. We may long for communion with our child and deeply grieve that which has passed; but we must work towards an acceptance of increased distance and separation, for in a very real sense these things are important parts of growing up.

Where, however, the child has sustained a serious viola-tion of trust, this normal pattern can be greatly exacerbated and the young person may *'exude an armoured, bounded, impenetrable aura, a steeliness that tries to lock out any trace of weakness or vulnerability. Even their language can manifest a cold, staccato tone'.*[19] They are extremely

---

17   Winnicott, ibid, p. 35
18   Winnicott, ibid. p. 64
19   Winnicott, ibid. p. 130

vulnerable, and revelation of their wounds, whilst they may long for it, fills them with dread. Even after their secret is told, survivors may continue to be very self-protective and private, sometimes even withdrawn; or they may exhibit the bravado so common in adolescence. We must take care how we approach them.

The revelation of wounds renders us all vulnerable. The covers, as Evetts-Secker suggests, are not to be ripped off; we are not to be gawped at by throngs of inquisitive eyes. No! We are not to be apprehended in this way. Why? There are a million reasons, but we need only point out that such behaviour merely replicates an experience of abuse. No wonder these young people reel at the thought of exposure. What to do? This? That? Yes? No? They are in torment and often do nothing. And if they do share their secret, those in whom they confide are plunged into a similar agony about what to do for the best.

One hundred years is a long time; not literal, of course; in fairytale-speak it refers to an indeterminate span of time before the spell is lifted. It is not set in stone. It will be when it will be. Until this happens, the hedge of thorn will keep out any that would venture forth. But when all is said and done, we also have to recognise that no one can keep a secret of this magnitude without cost to their souls.

Secrets cause a person to become haunted. She cannot sleep, for the secret is like a cruel barbed wire that catches across her gut as she tries to run free.[20]

So the search for the magic that will eventually lift the spell must proceed apace, for this is not a good state of affairs. Secret-keeping is a secondary burden to carry on top

---

20   Estes, ibid. p. 381

of the trauma of the actual event. As we have seen, it compromises all relationships, cutting survivors off from major sources of support: often those who love them most.

Maybe for a time secrets *are* necessary. Maybe time is needed to lick our wounds, alone or privately with close friends. Not to tell at all is the loneliest option of all and, sadly, the one that is chosen by millions of survivors. We were incredibly thankful that our child had been able to confide. We wished more than anything that it could have been with us, but recognised that her ability to break the silence saved her from the complete isolation experienced by countless silent others. The people she chose were for the most part sound individuals and, despite our distress at being left out, we felt proud of her choice of confidantes and certain that they did the best they could for her.

But can we really live an authentic life if those closest to us are oblivious to our pain, even with the best of motives? The lies that become increasingly necessary to fend off the truth erode and undo who we are. Telling lies is not easy, but the decision to keep a secret tragically necessitates them. It's part of a vicious and unrelenting trap that cages up great chunks of our lives, our spirits and ultimately even our souls. We register the looks of bewilderment on our loved ones' faces, see them struggling to make sense, picking up clues, scents, questioning; we register it all, feel their anxiety, their reaching out. But if we have a secret to keep, we must fend them off with all our might. It's not intentional, we don't mean any harm; but the fact remains that, like King Canute, we will do almost anything to hold back the tide.

A wise woman, writes Estes, *would draw the secret out, painful though it may be, for she knows that without tending, it makes a wound that will not heal.* [21]

Secrets are corrosive and if kept overlong can produce disturbing side-effects.

The danger for the adolescent is that if the wound is left unattended it can easily become split off from consciousness so that unconsciously one seeks outlets for anaesthetising the pain of which one is no longer aware. Alternatively, *the need to protect the wounded place from getting hurt again remains at the centre of one's consciousness and results in never allowing one's self to engage fully in life. In both cases consciousness remains wounded and bleeding.* [22]

Truth, when eventually it can be faced, is part of the healing, both for those who have kept a secret and for those who have been deceived. For when the truth is told we can start to work it through, come to terms, pull together, lick each other's wounds, get better, heal a little. In the end, revelation of the hurt will proceed in direct relationship to trust. With increased trust and patience would come glimpses of the daughter we knew still lived behind her defences.

As parents it took us a long time to arrive here. We grasped it intellectually fairly early on, but the estrangement came so suddenly and under such shocking conditions that our instincts went into overdrive. It was a long time before we were able to begin practising this more restrained and measured approach.

Along the way we had literally to transform ourselves. Everything had to be re-evaluated. And it got worse before

21   Estes, ibid. p. 377
22   Frankl 1998, p. 64-65

it got better. More than anything we wanted to be included in what was real; open up, not cover up and shut up. *There's nothing you can do until she's ready*, a friend finally insisted. She was herself a survivor of a sexual assault and understood completely where our daughter was coming from. Of course I knew this too but I absolutely hated to hear it. My heart sank. How many more locked doors? How many more brick walls? How many more impossible hedges of thorn?

But in the end I had to accept that, as a mother, I could not play the role of wise woman in relation to my child. I had finally to accept that maybe I would never know the truth of what had gone on in her life and that all I could really do was back off. Nothing to do but wait. Accept. Let go. Patience. When we cannot attend a wound directly, we must find a different approach, a new attitude. *New wine for new bottles.*[23] In the end, this new medicine would help us all to recover.

There is a kind of natural folk wisdom held amongst some groups of worldly-wise women that can shed light on this part of our story and upon our understanding of our own growing daughters. The wisdom relates to what is known as:

Stealing the key:

The moon was obscured that night, making the darkness blacker then ever; but it needed to be dark, otherwise the task could not be completed. It would not be easy for any of them, but it had to be done nevertheless. Mother was sleeping soundly when her young daughter crept into the room. Her hand trembled as she slipped it under the pillow and stole the precious key. When dawn broke, everything was changed.

---

23   Matthew 9: 17; Mark 2: 22; Luke 5: 37-8

It is a painful fact that daughters must of necessity wrench themselves free from their mothers during adolescence. The bond must be broken, the last psychic remnants of the umbilical chord severed. No one sees it coming, for this brutal separation is not part of the paradisaical myth of the mother-daughter relationship.

From the standpoint of the child, the psychological imperative is clear: the theft of the key is essential if the struggle for maturity and independence is to be won. Mothers, especially good ones (and this is their strength as well as the reason for their downfall), are reluctant to set their daughters free. Their reluctance is rooted in the instinct to protect; but it is a role which of necessity must be relinquished. A good daughter will effect a separation, however brutally, for she knows that in the end she must access the key that will unlock her own life.

It is a difficult transition for all concerned, not least the child, for the journey into adulthood inevitably involves the shattering of innocence. This can be tough enough even in 'normal' circumstances, but where the child has also experienced an abuse of trust it can be almost impossible to bear. The rug has been pulled out from beneath and, whilst in many ways it makes sense to call out for assistance, young people also need to find their feet for themselves. This need to survive by their own efforts, to get through something terrible by marshalling their own inner resources, is part of the important work of adolescence. When viewed organically in this way, the stress of sudden separation is significantly diminished.

We thought our lives as mothers would go on for ever. The emptiness is vast. Somehow we blinded ourselves to the facts of nature, to the inevitability of change. Yet we are promised new life in the future, if only we dare to grasp it – an issue to which I will return in a later chapter. But first we have to let go of our outmoded ways of being. The trick is knowing which parts have become obsolete and having the courage to let them go.

It's a dance. What I have learned from my experience thus far, and from the wise helpers that I have had the good fortune to meet, is that when we step back the results are miraculous. If we resist, we will simply become worn down, pursuing that which can only back off in response to our relentless pursuit. If we change the course of our steps, however, our world and our relationships will be transformed.

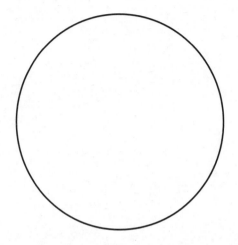

the full moon

calling the soul home
the centre of the dance

Calling the Soul Home

Dance reflects the patterns and threads of energy
which bring chaos into order,
on the cosmic as well as on the personal level. [24]

My daughter loves to dance. 'It's the only time I feel fully alive.' She has not said so directly, yet it is clear that dance is salve for her soul. My husband craves nature, long walks in the countryside, open space, making fires in a pot-bellied stove at the bottom of the garden late at night when we are all sleeping. I like to be quiet. Noise disturbs me. Mornings are best and sunsets, before and after the hustle of the day, when the light is soft and pink and you can hear the birds sing.

Everyone has a place that soothes, if only in the realms of imagination. After so much pain we need such things to sustain us. It's where we gather ourselves, reflect upon what has passed, what is to come; but it's also where we lose ourselves, where we stop thinking, striving, trying, and just 'be'.

---

24   Tom Chetwynd 1982, p. 112

There came a time when we simply had to accept this. So we downed tools and took a break for a couple of days in an English cathedral city. Winding down, we slowly began to regain a sense of ourselves. We knew it wasn't over but the weekend provided a much-needed recuperative space away from home. On our first afternoon we went to Evensong. The choir-boys sounded like angels, pure, lucid, youthful, magical, and we knew then just how far from the spirit we had strayed, how worn out and weary we had become.

Something changed that day, something I couldn't quite put my finger on; thinking now, I can see it was about hope. We had lost so much hope, you see. But being away from home, sitting at Evensong in a medieval church far away from our troubles, helped us to remember the people we had been before.

When we left the church the sun was setting. We walked hand in hand, something we'd not done for ages. That night after a long hot bath I lay in bed thinking over our day and how such a small change in environment, in atmosphere, could have such a soothing effect. I recalled the music of the choir from the afternoon and once more my mind fell upon the idea of angels. I remembered their first appearance in Dante's Divine Comedy. I pictured the Botticelli paintings of the hero's eventual rise from his long and tortuous sojourn through Purgatory. Could it be that such thoughts heralded something similar for us?

When we returned home I eagerly sought out The Divine Comedy and was surprised to discover that a guide had been present for Dante almost from the beginning of his journey, a guardian angel, walking beside him all the way, helping him to make sense of the terrible suffering he witnessed. However we think about such things (and there are many, many ways) the motif of a guardian angel enshrines and symbolises faith; faith that we are not alone, even in the deepest depths of our despair.

Whether angels exist or not is neither here nor there. Whether they be real or whether they represent a psychological or spiritual connection with what we might call 'source', what is abundantly clear is that to be divorced from these aspects of the creation, to be cut off, severed, exiled from their companionship, feels like being lost, utterly.

The juxtaposition of transcendence and entrapment mirrors a deep inner tension with which most of us struggle every day, a tension between two very different modes or aspects of being, two worlds and two perspectives from which to view our lives. One is connected to spirit, to the journey of the soul; the other, lost and abandoned in the wasteland, oblivious to the nature and meaning of the Quest. Two characters; the seeds of a story.

There's the one who knows: the angel, inner mentor, guardian, fairy godmother, the wise old woman in the forest who gives good counsel to the lost and frightened child, a higher aspect of the self, who understands the fullness of our story all the way from Once Upon a Time to Happily Ever After.

Then, however, there's the one who gets lost, the one who forgets, falls asleep, loses faith: the ordinary flesh and blood human being like you and me, the potential hero or heroine of story; and the core of myth and fairytale is centred around his or her struggle to find their way back home.

Those who have seen Wim Wenders' classic film 'Wings of Desire' will at once feel compassion for the predicament of both these aspects of the self: the one, overwhelmed by its own suffering, isolated, faithless, trapped in the depths of fear; the other, unseen and unheard yet seeing and hearing all. This one, feeling our feelings, monitoring our every thought from the most elevated and sacred to the most distressed and profane, is there through our despair, through the humdrum chatter of our minds, through birth and death and everything in between. Yet we behave as if we are alone, as if she or he were not there at all.

To imagine this plight, to have a glimpse into this world between worlds which Wim Wenders so poignantly illumines through the portal of his cinematic creation, is to come close, to touch the hem of the angelic garment, to feel the angelic burden, the mirrored exile from the very being whom she or he seeks to comfort, protect and guide back into the light. There is an unforgettable part of the film in which two angels stand unapprehended beside a suicidal man perched on the edge of a high-rise building in Berlin, intent upon ending his life. His mind races in turmoil. The angels hear all, offer thoughts of comfort, hope, faith, courage and forgiveness; but the suicidal man is utterly impervious and leaps instead to his death. There is nothing that the angels can do but watch.

So many of us have lived in exile from our angel. Pain has driven us from her hearth, from her old oak stump in the forest, from her candle-decked shrine in the church, her holy of holies in the ancient temple, our own spirits. But if only we will return, we will be assisted.

Rest, take a little time. Go off duty for a while. Be gentle with yourself. Re-acquaint yourself with the parts of your life that are quite fine. See what you have left: a sunset walk with a loved one, holding hands, music that soothes and uplifts your spirit; whatever you like, whatever you have, whatever you can dream. Gather these blessings to your heart, however small and insignificant they seem. In so far as we do, we will be released bit by bit from the curse that has seized our hearts. There are times when this is all that is required, a little remembering of goodness. For in its midst we are reconnected to our souls, and there is an angel walking by our side.

We can begin by opening our eyes, by gradually removing the shields that blind us to the fullness of our own selves, which includes the possibility of wings as well as tears. The benefits are great indeed; for to reconnect, to dare to see, to face our pain fully and still go forward, still live even in the midst of our own fragility, is truly to fly.

What is the knocking?
What is the knocking at the door in the night?
It is somebody who wants to do us harm.
No, no, it is the three strange angels,
Admit them, admit them. [25]

---

25   D. H. Lawrence, 1994

The Centre of the Dance

At the still point of the turning world...
... there the dance is ...
... except for that point, the still point,
There would be no dance, and there is only the dance.[26]

There, at the centre of the dance of creation, silence is. This elusive point – or one-pointedness, as the Buddhists would say – this centre of the lotus, if the creation be its flower, this stillness, is perfect peace. What emanates from this peace is in alignment with the divine, is the divine presence.

Life leads us astray from its source.

We can struggle all we like, exerting our own exiled will upon events in the external world; but unless we return to this source, all our efforts will have disappointing results. Phrases like 'I've lost the plot' or 'I'm on the edge' unconsciously describe our relationship, our distance from our own core. We have literally lost the paths to our own courts of joy, our inner Holy Grails. But they are there nevertheless. They have not ceased to exist, however hidden and obscured beneath the

26   T. S. Eliot 1944, line 62 ff

shadows of our lives. Very often we have to cut deep into the
blackness to find them; but it is a labour that can yield a
priceless treasure, for to find sanctuary in the midst of our
suffering, a place where we can rest and be at peace, is recuperative beyond our wildest dreams.

Yet what is this place, this lost Court of Joy, this
mythical Once Upon a Time that lies at the core of all our
stories, this land that never was and always is? And how
does one arrive there? It is said that it may be found under
the sea, through a magic mist, or upon distant islands east
of the sun and west of the moon. It may be known as
Avalon, Caer Siddi, the honeyed plane of bliss. Taliesin
sings of this Paradise:

> *O perfect is my seat in Caer Siddi,*
> *Nor plague nor age harms him who dwells therein.*
> *Manawyddan and Pryderi knew it.*
> *Three tuneful instruments around the fire play before it,*
> *And around its corners are ocean's currents,*
> *And the wonder-working spring is above it.*
> *Sweeter than white wine is the drink of it.* [27]

It is said that to drink from the Grail is to remember
paradise. But what is the purpose of this fleeting return to
source, this Holiday or Holy Day in the midst of all our
troubles? How shall we be assisted by the sip of paradise on
our tongues? Because, without re-connection, spiritually we
perish. The Grail is a sacred font, a breast, a life-giving flow;
energy, vitality, a magical blending of all that is and ever shall
be. Out of time – the pivot, nexus, centre of the dance.

Well, for seven years thereafter Taliesin and his
companions resided in this place. And they wanted for

---

[27] From an ancient Celtic text. See Matthews 1978, p.18

nothing and were full of joy. And, even though they had seen much sorrow, and even though they had suffered dearly themselves, they could remember nothing of this, nor of any other pain in the world. And the sweet birds of the Goddess Rhiannon sang to them throughout, and each song that they heard was more lovely than before and very soon they no longer noticed the passing of time.

But at the end of this wondrous span, one of the seven was tempted to open the forbidden door that leads back into the world. And when he looked, he remembered everything he had known there, and felt anew each and every loss and every bad thing that had happened to him, and every friend and loved one he missed. And from that same moment he could not rest, and straight away made haste from that place, which faded swiftly from view, like a dream of the soul.

Yet till the end of time it will remain in the Bardic prayer, that three times the number that would have filled the great ship Perdwyn – we entered into the deep and, excepting seven, none have returned.

So sang Taliesin, primary chief bard of Cymru, concerning the quest for the Cauldron of Inspiration known to us now as the Holy Grail. And whilst ever he sang, all the ills of those who heard were utterly dissolved. [28]

Whatever happens, there is always this place of stillness, this peace at the centre of the dance, at the centre of our souls. We must endeavour, if we are able, to remember the routes that lead back to such places; for, as the Celtic

---

28 See *The Mabinogion*, tr. Jones & Jones 1949, p. 39-40

mystics warn us, unless we find shelter in the midst of a storm, unless there is a place, deep in our hearts where we stay anchored, stay connected to God, we will lose our spiritual direction completely and be shredded to pieces.

So remember:

> *Even though we have only heard about, glimpsed, or dreamt of such a wondrous wild world that we once belonged to, even though we have not yet, or only momentarily, touched it, even though we do not identify ourselves as part of it, the memory of it is a beacon that guides us toward what we belong to, and for the rest of our lives.*[29]

---

[29] Estes, ibid. p. 187

the disseminating moon

reflections

the spindle

the predator: a cautionary tale

Persephones secret

Reflections

'A client once told me,' writes Jungian analyst Nor Hall,
'that she had dreamed the sentence:
"The moon contains the seeds of the process".'
By 'the process' she meant partly the arduous journey
toward relationship again and partly the process of
therapy, the recovery of self.
The moon contained the secret because of its periodic
nature: this woman who despaired over the loss of love …
knew that the wax and wane were a sign to live by.[30]

Now, the centre of the dance is the fullness of the moon; and the arrival at this place, this phase, this still, illuminated point within, precedes the second half of the lunar cycle, of the journey to a new moon and a new cycle of experience.

The cycle may be likened to a rhythmic dance of light and shadow in which the moon is revealed, concealed and revealed anew. Each phase of its procession through the night sky is perfectly mirrored in its opposite, so that what is concealed in the waxing is revealed in the waning and *vice versa*.

30   Nor Hall 1980, p. 23

In their opposition, at first so unbearable, we begin to
see a correspondence in the lunar phases, a relationship of
some sort. We see that, in a sense, they are partners in a
dance, sister images if you like. When looked at in this new
and previously obscured way, we can at last begin to fit the
phases together.

Now, if you would draw the cycle of the moon as it
appears at the start of this book and take a pencil to connect
the opposing phases, you will see, as I did, that together they
form perfect circles of light; full moons, if you like. It's as if
one is a question, the other its answer; as if the
interconnecting phases each have the capacity to explore
each other from seemingly irreconcilable perspectives. One
completes the other. But the relationships and correspondence
of the phases – the patterns, so to speak – only become clear
because of the increased consciousness characteristic of the
second half of the cycle; or, in different terms, of the later
and more developed stages of emotional recovery. Only then
can we see what we could not see before and in ways that
were utterly inconceivable at the time.

There is a sense in which the journey from Full to Dark
Moon reflects that which we have travelled from Dark to
Full; the most significant difference being, of course, that in
the latter we began from a position of 'darkness' as opposed
to the 'light' that now characterises our new point of departure.

> *Psychologically, the place of the full moon is the
> 'change of gears' point in the cycle – whatever occurs at
> this time is meant to help us become clear and objective
> to what has happened throughout the cycle thus far.*[31]

---

31   Dane Rudhayer 1971, p. 163

To transpose our story into the realms of the myth of Demeter and Persephone: in the nature of the mother's sorrowful wanderings we saw several stages of discovery, of revelation and response. We can surmise that the same was true for her daughter, though the terrain that Persephone surveyed was very different from that of her mother. Yet for a time both were deeply immersed in the blackness of the dark moon, itself *a paradigm of psychological depression.*[32]

This is a time of great confusion, as we have seen, and the dis-integrated psyche's first seemingly impossible task is to sort through all this confusion. Dis-integration refers to a state in which one's reality is reduced to fragments. The previous cohesion has been shattered. Both mother and daughter are torn to pieces. To re-integrate is to gather the fragments together to form a new whole. And if we are to bind all this brokenness together, if we are to elucidate the deeper meaning and significance of our loss, we, like Demeter, must eventually turn our gaze inwards and reflect upon ourselves. The revelations of the external world are clear. Now we must search for their meaning.

It is this reflective gazing that becomes the pre-occupation of Demeter as she waits for her daughter's return. This is the theme, the key signature that sets the tone for the final phases of her journey.

Now Demeter's transition, her process through these ever-changing phases of experience, is punctuated by three stopping-places. *All three are said to be portals into internal realms. The first is where her beautiful daughter disappears. It is a point where two worlds meet and where one can be cut off – literally, the cord has been cut and the daughter is gone.*[33]

---

32   Hall, ibid. p. 78
33   Hall, ibid. p. 78

So, veiled in dark robes, she sets forth searching; and for many days and nights she wanders in terrible grief and rage. She blights the crops, heaps blame upon her countrymen, her culture, even upon the gods themselves, until eventually, utterly exhausted, she collapses on the steps of the Maiden Well, the second point where it is said that the upper and lower worlds mingle and merge.

It can seem to those looking on that Demeter is defeated at this point, that she is broken in spirit, that she has at last become resigned to the fact of her loss. The latter is true but not the former. What has actually been constellated here is a shift in perception, a withdrawing of fixation upon the external world and a more conscious entry into communion with these inner realms of experience and meaning.

When we stand, so to speak, in the place of the full and newly-waning moon, we can look back at those early phases of uncertainty with the knowledge of hindsight revealed throughout the first hemicycle. This, of course, is an altogether different place. Time has passed; our emotions are not so raw. As the cycle progresses (to continue the metaphor), more and more distance is gained from the shock of the initial revelation and, if we are lucky, more and more insight will emerge, until finally we can let go and move on.

At the time of the dark and crescent moons, our tears were tears of confusion, bewilderment, shock, anger and disbelief. Tears shed in the full, however, have a very different quality from those shed throughout the waxing phases. They flow from compassion, acceptance, a renewed and gradually reintegrated faith.

Rites of Passage stories must of necessity first set a scene, a tone. Readers must be introduced to the predicament that initially stimulates the story into motion. But all such stories, if they are to dignify their intent, must move through and beyond their initial predicament. We cannot stay forever bemoaning our expulsion from paradise. We must at least attempt to resolve it in some way, so that we might arrive, as Eliot suggests, at a new beginning. Only then will we be set free.

So, as Demeter waits, she turns back the pages and reviews the story from the beginning; she sorts through the fragments, binds them together, however disjointed, into a reality she can work with, that she can endure. And as she withdraws more fully into herself, a shadow falls over her surface. Psychically she is re-visiting the other side of the moon.

But she has not gone away. Her disappearance into the night sky, like that of her daughter, is just a trick of the light.

Demeter's story raises issues, touched upon earlier, that sooner or later become pertinent to all mothers. These appertain to the inevitable separation and loss of intimacy that comes about at adolescence. We have seen the necessity from the standpoint of the child. Now let's have a look at the implications for the mother. How do we find the courage to disengage from our children as they mature, and what do we do with the gap left in our own lives as a result?

The myth shows that eventually Demeter withdraws her judgement around these matters. This does not mean that she condones the abduction of her daughter. Far from it; part of her is still defiantly holding out for Persephone's release from the underworld. But another part begins to tease out the broader meaning behind her separation from her child. This enables deeper vision.

The capacity to reflect without judgement, embodied by Demeter as she waits, denotes an important advance. It is a stopping-place along the road, from which we can view things in different ways and ask different sorts of questions, perhaps for the first time.

What did the beautiful daughter represent? What *part of the self* can no longer be found? Nor Hall explains that,

> *when the mother is separated unwillingly from her child or when the fruit is taken from her rather than given, a certain understanding is lost, an organic bond that severs the mother from her own life's meaning.*[34]

This is a crucial point to explore: this deep shock to the psyche that leaves her cast adrift from her life. A great part of my agony at that time was knowing that my child must have experienced the same deep shock to her psyche, the same ripping-away of certainty, security and trust that had characterised her life up to that moment.

Like our adolescent daughters, mothers too are thrust into a whole new realm. What we will each make of the new terrain cannot yet be fully known, but chances are the girl will eventually become a mother and her mother a grandmother. Life is full of transitions, of switching places, passing through phases.

I was where you are now.
You will be where I am.

And so the cycle turns. But it is not easy, continually being born, dying and finding new life. It is hard to be detached and accepting when the nights draw in, when the

---

34   Hall, ibid. p. 88

trees shed their leaves once so green and fresh and full of life, of hope for a future that will go on for ever. But time will turn, and suddenly (sometimes, it seems, so very suddenly) the summer birds are gathering on the rooftops, ready to fly away.

Go to your wide futures, you will cry if you are wise, even though your heart may be breaking. To say anything else is to fight against nature itself. At the same time we have to recognise that

> *it takes great strength to let go of a thing you have created – a child, a work of art, a string of words that work – but the estrangement, the giving up, the separations are often necessary in order for something fundamentally new to emerge.*[35]

The separation from one's child at adolescence can feel as powerful and as poignant as giving birth, when such a mammoth physical effort is required to release your child into the world. At adolescence the same effort is called for, but this time on a different level. Your world, like your womb, however paradisaical it might have been, however safe and secure and full of good things – and most probably it often was – by the end of a pregnancy, by adolescence, cramps and hems the child in; and the child is likely to be longing for another home in the world beyond your domain. A wise mother will willingly assist the child in these transitions. But separation is painful. Our hormones go wild; the transition rocks us to the core, even whilst we know its inevitability. Now our child is in the world, and vulnerable.

Within seconds of giving birth, a mother's instinct kicks in. If you have never felt it maybe you are lucky, for the intensity of love a parent feels for a new-born child is

---

35   Hall, ibid. p. 85

accompanied by an equally intense and overwhelming sense of responsibility. Just as much as you love, you will protect. You don't work these things out, you just know; and it's awesome.

This mother-instinct is designed to facilitate the perpetuation of our species; we have a sense of working with nature and our instincts serve a vital purpose. We feel aligned: aligned with our collective as well as our personal purpose. But when these first few years have passed and the child reaches puberty, the importance of the mother, of her instinct to nurture and protect, is no longer required in the same way. The trouble is that these deeply rooted instincts just don't go away.

For a time we have to learn to override them, sit beside them, honour them, trust; but it is no longer appropriate for us to act upon them as before. For, as we have seen, our adolescent children, who for the greater part of their lives have welcomed and relied upon our attentions, increasingly come to experience them as intrusive. For you see, far away on the other side of the moon, Persephone is learning how to look after herself; and this is just as vital, in the grand scheme of things, as it is for her mother to get in gear and step right back. Not so easy to see at first; yet in time this mother-instinct will ease its grip on our senses. In the meantime we must turn our attention elsewhere: to ourselves.

Our children will always be our children. We will always love and cherish them. But the application of our love must undergo a radical transformation as they mature. For us, the change came suddenly and in tragic circumstances, but the principal, the necessity of letting go is the same.

When the last child leaves home, the void is filled only
by the possibility of making something out of yourself. [36]

Now, as we remember, Demeter in her agony had caused
a bleak and barren winter to come upon the land. She had
withdrawn her gifts from her world, even from the gods
themselves. In the end, her defiance would fulfill an
essential role in securing her daughter's release from the
underworld but, as a reflection, we can see also that it was
her own self that had become barren. Cut off from her child-
bearing years, her role and identity as a mother had collapsed. And if not mother – what? The abduction of
Persephone underlines this pivotal transition in the sharpest
possible terms.

Look at the symbolism and this is clear. In a certain light
we can see that Demeter personifies the state of the world
when the soul is lost. She becomes for a time the embodiment
of the Wasteland; and Persephone – like the Holy Grail, like
the Sleeping Beauty – becomes a symbol of the lost soul. It
stands to reason then that, if the story is to proceed, Demeter
must eventually cease withholding *in herself*. She must find
the courage, even in her exile, to allow time to turn once
more; she must accept change, no matter how painful. When
she does, when she dares to bring forth another spring, to
bless rather than blight her world, things move toward
resolution at a rapid pace.

The twist in the tale, you see, is that Demeter must
rediscover the maiden in herself. She must return to the
experience of joy in the midst of loss, however impossibly
difficult this may seem, just as Persephone, through her
own initiation, must experience the darkness of the underworld before she fully becomes a woman; before she
returns to the world above.

---

36   Hall, ibid. p. 85

There is a unity to their story, as one might expect from such an ancient mythological outpouring. Everything does connect, like the opposing phases of the lunar cycle. Mother and daughter are engaged in an eternal mystery of transition, in which both of them experience total discontinuity from what was known and trusted. The promise of the story is that, by and by, mother and daughter will be reunited. A new cycle will eventually commence, and it is this sure knowledge that sustains Demeter through the final stages of this difficult journey.

The Spindle

'For fifteen years to the very day.
There will be no price to pay.
But on that day when you have no care,
she shall wander alone up a winding stair.
And there in the darkness we shall meet.
My task will almost be complete.
Spinning Wheel and Silver Thread,
She'll be pierced by a spindle and fall down dead.'

This terrible spell, cast by the Thirteenth Fairy at the Sleeping Beauty's *christening party, was quickly softened by the Twelfth Fairy who instantly stepped forward to reassure the distraught King and Queen that things were not as bad as they seemed.*

Although it is true what my sister has said
Beauty will prick her finger, but she'll not fall down dead.
Death will not claim her, so dry your tears.
Instead she will sleep for one hundred years.

Remember, Remember, Remember.

I want to explore this story further now, reflecting upon it more fully to see what it might reveal about the shutdown that occurred in our wider circle of family and friends in response to the crime.

As we have seen, fairytales can be read on many levels simultaneously. The idea is that these levels are mysteriously connected and fused with one another, so that what is true for the individual may also true for the family and the wider culture. In this story we see that when the young princess falls asleep, the entire court of characters fall asleep around her. We have already touched upon the tale in relation to the princess at its heart. My intention here is to tease out what it may say about the other characters and the kingdom into which the princess was born. So I hope you will bear with me as I attempt to unravel some of this wider symbolism.

The spindle, of course, is crucial, an obvious masculine symbol that causes a piercing, a deep wounding that plunges everyone into a deep sleep. But at the start the king and queen were blissfully ignorant about what lay ahead. On that fateful day fifteen years later, when their beautiful daughter was allowed to explore the palace all alone, they were preoccupied. The absence of the parents is a theme common in mythological material, an important thread in the rich weave of such stories. Somehow the stage is left open for the emergence of a challenge. But for the moment let's return to the beginning:

There was so much joy around the birth of the little princess. You see, the king and queen had waited such a long time for this child – she was the answer to all their prayers, all their longings. The day of her christening was declared a public holiday and the happy peal of church bells rang out across the land.

Births are new beginnings, and the birth of a princess signifies new beginnings for the group, for the kingdom as a whole. The ringing of bells proclaims this. It is interesting to note that the king and queen had experienced difficulty in conceiving this child. This is our first clue as to the state of the kingdom before she arrived; clearly there was already a weakness, a problem of some sort, as if the values that the princess would come to represent could not easily be 'conceived'. But when she was born, it seemed as if the problem had gone away and every one was beside themselves with joy.

It is said that the queen was quite serene after the birth, quietly tending to her daughter's needs, as young mothers often do. It's as if we can't quite believe the miracle that's just occurred in our lives. We stare at our new-borns in utter delight, soothing their every discomfort, cosseting and crooning as though we'd been given a little Buddha to look after. We immerse ourselves completely in the new relationship. Worldly events such as parties do not have the same allure.

Fathers generally respond in much more practical ways. This is certainly how the king behaved in this particular tale. At first bowled over by the birth of his daughter, he very quickly got himself into another gear, a gear outside the feminine realm. He had a real dependant now and he acted in a way as instinctual to him as the mother role was to the queen. Whilst she must immerse herself in the world of her child, at least until her offspring was weaned, he became driven by the need to provide and protect. In order to do this he had to return to the ordinary, everyday world far sooner than she.

And of course, someone had to organise the christening!

It seems significant that the problem re-surfaced at a family gathering. Births, deaths, marriages, birthdays; all family anniversaries and celebrations are quintessentially about remembrance. We stand back, review the past and gaze hopefully into the future.

Not surprisingly, therefore, they are often characterised by the re-appearance of the family shadow, the ancient curse, the weakness in the group. The dysfunctional aspect of the whole, whose faint echo sounded at the beginning, returns like a slap in the face.

Conflict does not erupt out of the blue. It arises because what should be part of the whole is somehow denied or forgotten. The Thirteenth Fairy couldn't just *not come*, you see; she couldn't just decide to take it all philosophically and not respond to the fact that she hadn't been invited. In fairy lore, as well as in matters of the psyche, this simply isn't an option. Thirteen fairies must be present, so to speak, at every child's christening. And the role ascribed to an *invited* guest is very different from that of an uninvited one; the latter, by the very nature of things, must bring everything that is denied and disowned.

There was nothing intrinsically wicked about this fairy – it could easily have been one of her sisters – but she drew the short straw and became for the duration the embodiment of the curse that was to befall them all.

Now, the fairies had not been in the least surprised by the missing invitation. They had been watching the story unfold from behind the scenes and had wondered which of them would end up being forgotten. The odds were rather high on it being the Thirteenth, for all sorts of reasons. Her sisters had consoled her in advance and bucked her up as best they could.

'What a difficult role, dear,' they said. 'You'll have to go anyway and do what has to be done, but we don't envy you. You won't be able to give the gift you wanted and you'll have to speak the fated words that will make the king and queen shudder in their shoes. The princess will certainly cry too. Not an enviable role at all.'

But being fairies, with their famous far sight, they could see it would all turn out well in the end. The mortals, however, had no such consolation. The Queen wept, the princess sobbed, even after the Twelfth Fairy had softened her sister's spell; for one hundred years seemed an awfully long time to be asleep.

The king hated all this weeping. He felt so responsible, you see. He wanted more than anything to put things right. That's when he came up with the plan of banishing all the spindles. As soon as the fairies had left, he issued a decree forbidding their possession on pain of death. All were hastily rounded up and burnt in huge fires in town squares across the kingdom. But inevitably one such spindle remained undiscovered, hidden in a dusty room at the top of a derelict tower in the castle grounds. Precisely where the innocent princess arrived on the day of her fifteenth birthday.

The more we study this story, the more it becomes clear that the king's way of dealing with problems was to employ an overly logical response. But this is not based on wisdom, and in the end creates unforeseen consequences for the very daughter he was trying to protect. Now, in fairytale speak, the King is a symbol, as indeed are all the characters. He represents that which is dominant in the whole: the attitudes and core values prevalent in family and kingdom. Clearly, these values are masculine and rational, normally associated

with the left brain. After all, he only had twelve golden plates
– only twelve possibilities to admit to his consciousness, so
to speak. He forgot to invite the thirteenth fairy, who
represents the complementary feminine values of feeling
and intuition associated with the right brain. But she came
anyway, full of rage, as we have seen.

The king does not intend to cause problems, but they are
created nevertheless, for an over-preponderance of rational-
ity divorced from feeling always creates havoc in the psyche. His logic tells him that the best way to protect his child
is by banishing all aspects of life that posed a threat. The
tragedy   is   that   the   trouble   keeps   escalating
precisely because of this banishing and splitting behaviour:

> *any split, if perpetuated, becomes an evil, something*
> *that is broken. But the idea is that it can be put together*
> *again and made whole; then something is gained, a new*
> *consciousness or a new stage of evolution.* [37]

The princess represents this new stage of evolution, in
herself and also for the group; for it is she who, in ignoring
the dominant consensus, seeks out the dusty room at the top
of the tower. She is curious and innocent. But what she
discovers there is so shocking that she is struck down and
silenced for one hundred years. She falls victim to the
ancient curse, but in the end she becomes the heroine of the
story, for without her there could be no opportunity to put
the kingdom in order. But first she must meet her nemesis.

It was very dark in the little room and at first the
princess saw nothing. But as her eyes adjusted to the
dim light, she saw an old, old, woman, bending over a
strange-looking wheel.

---

37 Chetwynd, ibid. pp. 379-380

'Come in my dear,' she whispered, beckoning the child toward her. 'Do you know what I am doing?'

'I do not,' replied the girl. 'I have never seen such a contraption before. What is it?'

'It is a spindle my child, the only one left in the whole land, and I am spinning my fine silver thread upon it. Would you like to try?'

The princess was fascinated and eager to try for herself. But no sooner had she sat down to spin than she pricked her finger and fell down upon the cold stone floor.

To prohibit, to forbid, to drive underground or up the tower, does not in the end achieve the desired result. For what we banish does not cease to exist but falls into shadow where, through lack of communion with the whole, it becomes darker and less benign.

Spinning-wheels and Thirteenth Fairies were integral parts of the culture. Their removal had implications. Symbolically the spinning-wheel was at the hub of the productive life of the feminine realms of experience. It was within this banished domain that the princess would have learned the secrets of her sex, its joys and sorrows, powers and vulnerabilities. For to spin and to weave, on whatever level, are quintessentially feminine activities, and the spinning-wheel symbolises the rightful occupation of the soul. It is deeply meditative and creative and should have been a vital part of Beauty's education. But no one in the kingdom under the age of fifteen had ever seen, let alone learnt to use one. Most of them probably didn't want to; possession was a serious offence. In consequence, the kingdom had become separated from its creative centre. Nothing could thrive thereafter, nothing could breathe, the feminine soul could not find its voice and in the end fell silent.

The positive masculine component of the psyche and the group, the positive animus, to use Jung's term, was far away. The prince who would eventually come to awaken them is not even in the frame and would not make his appearance until one hundred years were past and gone.

The kingdom is in a state of stagnation, sterility, because its masculine and feminine halves cannot relate.[38]

But, as we have seen, there was no consciousness around this danger. By their daughter's fifteenth birthday, the king and queen appeared to have forgotten the terrible prophecy. It would seem as if they were already sleeping, or at least not paying attention. Such was the king's level of trust in the ability of rational reason to save the day. All the spindles had been destroyed, hadn't they?

Some say the Queen hadn't been sure about the wisdom of all the banishing and burning, and about not having invited the Thirteenth Fairy, but had allowed herself to be persuaded. Interesting, don't you think? As if her basic wit, her intuition as to what really constituted a danger, was not fully valued by those around her, and so it was difficult for her to value it in herself. Had she been able to stand her ground, to help her husband find a different way, things might have worked out better.

It's not difficult to imagine how it might have been had the king invited the Thirteenth Fairy in the first place and to hazard a guess at what her gift might have been. We don't have to try very hard, for when the princess's birthday arrives we see clearly that it's the very thing she has been forbidden – the spindle – and all the disowned life it represents.

---

38   Chetwynd, ibid. pp. 379-380

Had she been invited and her gift given, as intended, in a positive, wholesome way, the princess would probably not have come upon it so negatively later on. But because she had never seen a spinning-wheel, because she had had no tuition in its use, she did not know how to proceed, did not apprehend its *dangers*. Suddenly she was in an unknown and forbidden dimension (her father's greatest fear) and in an instant she was lost to its dark and sinister power.

It seems so unfair that it falls to this lovely, innocent child to discover these hidden things, and yet, for there must be hope in every story, it is good that she does discover them, even though she loses her innocence forever. For, as she sits down to spin, she breaks the thread that will ultimately free them all. But the cost is high: she is wounded and bleeds.

The symbolism of blood is important on several levels, signifying the onset of puberty, the important transition from childhood, but also the tie between family members. The blood connects them to one another and also, as Chetwynd explains to, *'the inner life, the inner truth'*.[39] The princess's wound connects her to the hitherto obscured truth about her family and the kingdom in which she lives. The good news, though hard to see at the time, is that this problem can be addressed. For now, no one can hide from it any more. But, and this is what so often happens in fairytales, as well as in ordinary life, the situation gets much worse before it gets better: just at the moment when the curse comes into view, as it were, and all the pieces start fitting together and a new meaning starts to emerge, everyone suddenly falls asleep and a huge thorny hedge springs up around them. What was discovered is quickly repressed again, and it's left to those on the outside to fathom a solution.

---

39   Chetwynd, ibid. p. 377

The fairies of course are immortal, outside the normal constraints of time. One hundred years to them is but a wink of an eye. They stand aside from the drama like the gods of Olympus, watching it unfold. Those who live closest to the forest – the poets and the storytellers – have inklings and imaginings, as we have said. They make up the story of the sleeping princess and pass it on so that nothing gets truly forgotten and, crucially, because someone might hear and know what to do.

Those further away, however, thought their story highly improbable and gradually became convinced by more popular and frightening accounts that said the place was haunted by evil spirits. And, fearing, everyone kept well away, and the forest grew taller and taller and the brambles became ever more entangled until in the end even the turrets of the palace towers, with their royal flags and family crest on top, could no longer be seen.

The symbolism of sleep, so central to this story, expresses this unconsciousness and unrelatedness. Every-one hidden behind is still alive, but somehow stuck. No-one has died, but what we see here is a kind of living death. The characters are frozen, petrified, unable to proceed with their lives. Dialogue and reflection among themselves and with those on the outside is no longer possible. The dominant values remain unchallenged. The beautiful princess at the heart of the matter is unable to realise her creative birthright or her union with the conspicuously absent prince. On the outside, time still turns, the seasons come and go; but within nothing stirs, nothing changes. They are in a perpetual inter. The curse they thought they could cheat has had its way. But this time, it has grown in potency and now puts a halt to all their lives.

There is a sense in which this sad configuration depicts the impact and consequences of tragedy as it occurs in real life, when family members are unable to communicate with one another. We must endeavour to get behind the scenes to see what's really going on. But it's much easier said than done, for this is where all the hurt is, the ancient wounds from long ago. And surrounding all this hurt, these deep, ancient wounds, are the constructs, conscious or otherwise, that we have put in place like Sleeping Beauty's hedge of thorn for fear of getting hurt again.

The Sleeping Beauty is the central symbol of this wounded soul, cut off from others as well as herself. It seems there is no possibility of redemption, for one hunded years, because all the significant people in her life have fallen asleep around her. Are they not all Sleeping Beauties, all wounded by the same curse that is in some way specific to their grouping, as is the thorny hedge that has so mysteriously sprung up around them?

That these thorns resemble the spindle reveals a difficult but important truth about human nature. We defend in the same way as we have been attacked. We injure in the same way as we were injured and ensnare in the same way as we were ensnared. If you have ever tried to pass through a part of the forest that has become overgrown with bramble and briar, you will know first-hand how it is practically impossible to do so without getting wounded or ensnared.

We have seen how effective such defences are at keeping out those who come with the wrong attitude. But it is also true that when a soul is distressed, the defences keep out *all* who would approach, however they come. Maybe we can say in this instance that the soul has temporarily lost its power to discriminate. A blanket reaction has sprung into place around the wounded area and no one, friend or foe, can pass.

It seems reasonable to speculate that one of life's lessons for a person or group so defended is to learn the very necessary skill of *discrimination*. It is essential to apprehend danger, to protect oneself from intrusion and harm. This is a given. But discrimination is the real key, the real wisdom. And an attack highlights the possibility that this skill may not have been properly taught within the family or group.

It is up to each of us to explore these issues within ourselves, to see when and where we have deployed our defences accurately and for sound reasons and when and where we have closed our hearts needlessly. Where have we closed in on ourselves like the petals of a rose until all that can be seen are the thorny stems from which fragrant blooms once sprang? Often, we are not even aware when we shut down or attack in these ways, but a sure sign that we have lost our own heart connection is where there is coldness in our response to benign others. For coldness is the greatest distancer of all and the surest sign that something is gravely amiss within.

Now, in the Quest for the Holy Grail, we come at this theme from a slightly different angle: here at the centre of the forest a King lies terribly wounded. He can neither die nor find relief from his torment. In the Sleeping Beauty, on the other hand, the young princess may be seen in relation to her father as an *aspect* of the King and his kingdom. We see behind the masculine defenses to the feminine, child-like self within, whose essential needs have been dishonoured and silenced, just like those of the once-radiant Grail Maiden.

In essence, it's the king and the kingdom that are sick, not primarily the princess. That is why, in the Grail Quest, the elixir of the Holy Cup must first be served to the king. Then like a miracle, the dishonoured maiden of that legend and the wastelands that surround her will be restored and made whole. In the Sleeping Beauty, this miracle will coincide with the arrival of the prince.

To sum up, it is clear that the group in which the injury occurs is highly meaningful. This is no isolated incident, but inextricably bound up with a much more ancient pattern, in the blood so to speak, like the genetic code. Family illnesses get passed from generation to generation but if we know about them, we can live lives that minimise our susceptibility. When we don't know, we are powerless to help ourselves.

This is the consciousness we need, individually and collectively, to bring to bear on these patterns in order that the family curse may be lifted, once and for all. On one level then, and there are many, many levels to these mysteries, the Sleeping Beauty is about what happens when the feeling and intuitive sides of life are undervalued. The goal is that one day the estranged sides will find a way to reconnect, acknowledge and learn from one another. For this to occur, both must be acknowledged and integrated.

Only then will the spell be lifted; and, incidentally, only then will it become clear that the Thirteenth Fairy wasn't fundamentally evil after all! The truth is, she had something important to tell them. The palace did rock to its foundations and the window panes did shatter and crash to the floor. Had she been invited, it would have been a different story. She was not the danger, just the one warning against it.

P. L. Travers, in her adaptation of the story, writes that the Thirteenth Fairy stayed awake throughout all the dark years of sleep, when nothing stirred in the wood, spring never came and the sun never shone. Her heart bled at the sight of them all lying there, asleep and unconscious. She waited for the conception and birth of the princely hero in a far-off land, and then led him by her invisible promptings to travel to the sleeping kingdom and discover the Sleeping Beauty at its heart.

Surely in the end her difficult position will be understood as integral to the plot and she, like all the rest, will be forgiven and released into another dawn, another day, another part to play. (Maybe something less complicated: the fairy godmother in Cinderella? I've never read a word against her!)

We all have a little bit of the Thirteenth Fairy in us; self, family and culture alike. There's a Sleeping Beauty too, an innocent self who has experienced a painful initiatory wound and fled behind a thorny hedge. And most definitely there's something of the overly rational king, as well as the distraught, ineffectual queen and an entire court of colourful characters that for the moment still lie sleeping.

So in the end, *and* in order to proceed, we must be brave and set forth into these thorny woods like the heroes before us. We must become our own gentle princes, who come when the time is ripe, our own knights of the Grail, who find their way through to the wounded soul at its heart. We will need courage to proceed, for the path to her door leads through realms of deepest darkness where nothing is as it first appears; but we must hold our courage and make the attempt nevertheless, for beyond there is indeed a living rose.

Remember, Remember, Remember

The Predator:
a Cautionary Tale

All creatures must learn that there exist predators.
Without this knowledge a woman will be unable to
negotiate safely within her own forest
without also being devoured.
To understand the predator is to become a mature animal.[40]

In this chapter I want to take the unusual step of introducing a character from a fairytale not discussed thus far. Though this may seem to undermine the carefully worked out structure and balance of the piece, it is precisely what can happen in real life too, even with our best-laid plans. Something that does not fit arrives and threatens our safety. The new character, Bluebeard, is a dangerous predator.

His is the kind of story that Beauty might have listened to whilst she was spinning and weaving, if spinning and weaving hadn't been forbidden. It's a teaching story, like all the rest, but this one is specifically designed to equip the innocent with the wit they need to survive in the grown-up world. But, of course, Beauty never got to hear such a story and was woefully unprepared as a result.

Now, unlike the old King in the preceeding tale, who

---

40   Estes, ibid. p. 363

found it so difficult to value the essential feminine qualities and kept pushing them away without realising they were the things that could have helped most, the character of Bluebeard is much more sinister. The King's crime was his ignorance. His intentions were sound. In contrast, Bluebeard is full of evil cunning and his intention is not to protect but to undo the innocent girl at the heart of the story in the most dastardly of ways. He slips into the equation unapprehended, because of the deficiency in the consciousness of the whole.

Deep down in our bones, we all have the capacity to apprehend danger, but it needs to be nurtured and developed, paid attention to, made conscious. For if it is not, those who would harm us, on whatever level, will use this lack of consciousness to their advantage. Somehow they can sense we are not fully alert; they hone in, like the dark characters of fairytale.

Innocence so precious is open to theft, no matter how old we are.

It is with tender hearts that we lament its passing, but without wit and cunning the innocent will not survive. This is as true in the animal world as it is in our own, where naïvety, injury and open wounds attract predators. The relationship between predators and their prey is part of the complex dance of creation. They are drawn to one another unconsciously, so in order to remain safe, in the broadest possible sense, we must become acquainted with those parts of ourselves that still feel they are living in paradise. We are not.

We need to assist our children, not through cosseting and fear-mongering but through the deliberate cultivation of alertness, connectedness, intuition, sensation, feeling. Most pack animals can smell an intruder even at the extreme outer periphery of their territory. Every hair on their bodies stands on end, their glands send adrenaline streaming through their veins, other members of the group are instantly alerted, and all before the intruder is even sighted. These basic instincts, necessary for survival, are the rightful possession of every animal on the planet, including us. They not only protect us from danger but they also substantially enhance our effectiveness, fulfilment and freedom to live as we choose.

To re-actualise these innate gifts we need to pay attention to our capacity to predict at lightning speed, using our gut response, not to 'act nice', if so acting is not appropriate, and to draw up firm boundaries if the need arises. Easier said than done, especially when we realise that perhaps our own ability to read our environs is not all that it might be. Instead of getting caught into the deadly charm of it, on whatever level, we must put our attention firmly on our gut. It knows!

In more serious situations we may need to cry out. The sad thing is that we are often in too deep before we realise what is happening. We have mistrusted our own forebodings and rendered ourselves open to attack. The vast majority of assaults on children are committed by people they know, trusted adults, often within the family where they have every right to feel safe. We are off-guard in these situations, parents and children alike. We are more vulnerable than ever. But trust must never be based on blind faith.

Threat is diminished in proportion to the level of our awareness. If we're awake, alert, we cease to broadcast our vulnerability, and that in essence is our ultimate defence, our protection, our inviolate space. Ultimately, our safety and security in the world is the gift of consciousness. Nothing more, nothing less.

The mustering of the strength and wisdom to proclaim *this far and no further* [41] in our dealings with the external world is vital to our safety.

But what about the ability to make the same proclamation on an inner level? Surely this is where we must now shift our focus. Eventually, says Clarissa Pinkola Estes, we must all contend with *the predator within our own psyches*. Increasing awareness of this inner predator is crucial, for in some mysterious way our ignorance of its existence can create a chink in our basic defences through which an external predator may easily break through.

To elucidate this idea, Estes prescribes the fairytale of Bluebeard: he who extinguishes the light in a person's soul, pours scorn, belittles, entraps big-time. So we'd better take a deep breath, look with as much courage as possible at the devastation that such a presence can bring about and act promptly to save our souls.

Now in the deepest, darkest dungeon of Bluebeard's castle there is a hidden room. The door is obscured and tightly locked – for within lies a terrible and sickening truth.

By and by Bluebeard woos a young girl and in time she becomes his wife. She is not the first to travel this path, but unlike her own sisters, who are a little older and wiser, she is pure and innocent and does not yet know the wickedness of the world. When he charms her she shuns the warnings of her sisters, who are repelled by his attentions.

So first we need to pay attention to our sisters within. They are really on our side.

---

41   Estes, ibid. p. 363

Time passes, and eventually Bluebeard announces that he must go away for a while. He tells his young wife that her sisters may stay with her whilst he is gone, and before he leaves he hands her a collection of keys and says she may visit all the rooms in the castle except one.

After his departure the young girl and her sisters set off on their explorations. They eventually come to the dungeon and with the last remaining key, unlock the hidden door – and that is when they see the terrible secret within.

In the Grail legends, this room corresponds in part to a similar little chamber, deep within the enchanted realms, where Sir Percival first sees the wounded king who can neither die nor seek relief from his torment. In the Sleeping Beauty, it corresponds to the dusty room at the top of the tower. But in the Bluebeard story, it is harrowing in the extreme, for it hides the slaughtered corpses of all his previous wives. Finally the young girl understands the grim fate that her husband has in store for her.

If we imagine that each of these women represents the thwarted hopes and dreams of parts of our creative selves, as Estes suggests, we shall come close to the inner meaning of this harrowing motif.

It is the worst possible discovery to make, perhaps even more shockingly on an inner level. Even though we understand that the figure of Bluebeard is but a personification of an energy within our internal worlds, the shock of discovery is enough to make us vomit. The resonance, if there is any, makes it worse, for it confirms that such a force may be secretly attempting to undo our most sacred aspirations.

This internalised, introjected or innate negativity must be attended to. The good news is that getting on to the predatory force is the first step towards liberation. A hidden enemy is much more dangerous than a visible one. Even if all we can do is become more conscious of its exploits, this is a massive step forward.

The curiosity of the sisters leads them to this dark discovery. If they hadn't been so nosy, the youngest would almost certainly have ended up a victim. So they must be commended; as must we be for daring to explore even the dungeons of ourselves. What they discovered there was horrific in the extreme, but without consciousness we are all easy prey.

Fairytales provide excellent maps. In this case they show us precisely how to stand up to such a powerful, negative force. They are worth paying attention to because unless we start neutralising this destructive power within, it will for ever undermine our lives.

In the quest for the Holy Grail, the healing of the Wasteland turns upon the ability to ask the right question.

Asking the proper question is the central action of transformation – in fairytales, in analysis and in individuation. It is at this point that the naïve nature begins to mature, to question, 'What lies behind the visible? What is it that causes that shadow to loom upon the wall?[42]

Questions such as these are keys that unlock the truth. Sometimes such keys are stolen, as we have seen; at others they are given with dastardly intent.

---

42   Estes, ibid. pp. 48-49

To unlock the forbidden chamber is to commence one's initiation into the deepest, darkest secrets of the psyche, in this case something that mindlessly degrades and destroys a woman's potential.[43]

Somehow, those who undermine us in our outer worlds tune into this dispossessed place within and use it to dishonour us. The combination creates a nightmarish dance.

The longer the internal predator is hidden the more dramatic and more devastating the external manifestations will be, until in the end we are plunged into some sort of life crisis. The Chinese symbol for crisis has two meanings: danger and opportunity. Difficult to assimilate, from a western cultural standpoint, but more and more we are being encouraged to embrace the opportunities that crises often bring.

So after the door to the secret room has been unlocked we must be brave. We should, if we are able, pick ourselves up off the floor and resist the temptation to collapse. Easier said than done, for the sheer sight of the carnage within is enough to divest us on the spot of all vitality. Yet we need every scrap of wisdom we can rally, now more than ever. For this is the moment, says Estes, when the heroine must ask the pivotal question. If we fail at this point we, like Sir Percival, will be plunged back into the trackless wastes of the forest.

It is pertinent to consider, when reviewing such stories, that not all characters succeed or even survive. We saw clearly, in the story of Sleeping Beauty, the fate of many brave knights, those who came at the wrong time or with the wrong attitude, hopelessly caught and trapped within the thicket, their skeletal forms hanging from the trees,

---

43   Estes, ibid. p. 47

mirroring the piles of slaughtered women in Bluebeard's dungeon. We must, if we are able, follow in the tracks of the heroines and heroes of these tales. But of equal importance, we must heed the warnings, the cautions that other more peripheral characters represent.

The symbolism of the slaughtered wives suggests a state of suspended animation, similar to the Sleeping Beauty motif but in a much more sinister form. Here, the soul is not merely sleeping but has been deliberately drained of vitality, of life, in a deeply demonic and vampirish kind of way.

Those who are wise know about the predator within a woman's psyche as well as in her external world. What is sometimes difficult for us lesser mortals to grasp is the interplay between these dual realities. We may think we have cleaned up our act; God knows we have tried. But there is always more work to be done, more hidden rooms within the psyche to be discovered; even Bluebeards on the loose. And as Estes points out, *the deeper we go, the darker and more difficult the terrain.* There is something about a crisis that forces our hand; but in a good way, a way that, although we cannot see it at the time, is necessary for the soul. Tough medicine, but true.

Now, in the Bluebeard story, what lies within the hidden room is so shocking that the sisters slam the door shut as quickly as they can. But once the secret is out, it can no longer be contained. There is blood on the key, *'not menstrual blood, but arterial blood from the soul.'* [44]

Whatever the sisters do they cannot scrub it clean, cannot stop it bleeding. How they wish it were not so! How they wish they had not opened the forbidden door and, oh, how desperately they try to hide it!

44   Estes, ibid. p. 51

This is a common reaction, but it's not the best response. The more grown-up parts of us know this, know that the hidden reality must be brought into the light. But the sisters still scrub and clean, to no avail whatsoever, for when Bluebeard returns the leaking blood betrays them.

The only goal worth considering at this point is escape, but first they must rally themselves against Bluebeard, who is now confirmed beyond all doubt as the predator. This is *not* the moment to 'act nice'!

When a woman understands that she has been prey, both in the outer and inner worlds, she can hardly bear it. It strikes at the root of who she is at centre and she plans as she must, to 'kill' the predatory force.[45]

While ever we are ignorant, innocent of the predator's true intentions, he maintains a position of power within the psyche. While ever we buy in to his debilitating charm, to his threats, he is lord of the castle. At this point, those aspects of the self who would normally come to our aid, those that would see through to his cruel heart, are not even in the frame. But once the illusion is broken and the girl sees the predator's true colours, the dark charm with which he entraps her is broken and immediately she begins to act in her own best interest.

In response to this wizening, Bluebeard becomes enraged and screams at her that she has '*violated the holy of holies and must now die*'.[46]

But now that she is clued up to his warped inversions of the truth that serve only his predatory intentions, she cunningly lulls him into a false sense of security by asking

45   Estes, ibid. p. 56
46   Estes, ibid. p. 56

for time to prepare for her death. This is her first mature act. Her second is to use this precious time to call forth assistance: her own masculine psychic muscle. In this story, this positive masculine component of consciousness is represented by her brothers, whom she bids her sisters call forth from the parapet of the castle.

At first they are far away – too far, as Estes points out – and this is possibly the reason why the young women have found themselves so unprotected, so open to the predatory force. But as the sisters' cry gathers momentum it begins to travel, until eventually it is heard in the place where the brothers live, in the place *where those aspects of the psyche that are trained to fight, to fight to the death if necessary, live*.[47]

Soon they are galloping toward the castle to assist her, and they arrive in the nick of time to save her from her fate.

Bluebeard is slain.

No questions; no negotiations; no dialogue. Just slain.

What we see here is a combination of aspects or qualities working together. The sisters' re-found wit and ingenuity and the brothers' brute strength and humanity together produce a recipe that finally overwhelms the predator, deposes him and puts an end to his wicked ways.

Several months after the secret came out, I had a distressed call from my eldest daughter. She told me about a dream she had had the previous night. She was being shown round a house that a friend was renting. At first her mind was full of everyday preoccupations but gradually, as she ascended several flights of stairs, the atmosphere became dark and when she came to the top floor she discovered a frail, bruised and frightened girl, huddled in a little cupboard.

There was a menacing presence nearby but she did not know what. She picked up the girl, who was deceptively heavy, and started to carry her to safety downstairs. But as she descended the stairs, the scenery began to change and by the time she reached the ground floor, she was back home, in our own front room. We have a large bay window looking out over the street and as she entered the room she saw the perpetrator of the crime lurking ominously outside. She laid the girl, who had mysteriously changed into her younger sister, out of his sight in between two sofas. She then gave out a most anguished cry. At that moment I suddenly appeared on the street, took a gun out of my pocket and shot him.

Dreams are complex carriers of images that reflect the dreamer's interior world as well as her external one. We have all been laid low by the crime against our family member (on some level we are all frail and broken children) yet we each have the potential to be the rescuer too, to carry our wounded selves to safety, to protect them thereafter and, like 'the brothers', put an end to the destructive actions of the predator.

The shooting, like the slaying of Bluebeard, is a metaphor. No-one is being killed literally, even though such crimes bring our blood to boiling point. What is happening here is that the actions of the predator, on *an internal level*, are being divested of energy, divested of capacity to prey, to entrap, to suck the marrow out of our very bones. This is the fate of Bluebeard and also that of the predator in my daughter's dream.

Fairytales are full of motifs where the heroine or hero must distinguish between those characters who are easily redeemable and those who are not, those who for the sake of the whole must be dealt with differently. The beast in Beauty and the Beast is one such figure. He looks ugly on the outside but inside he's gentle, loving and courteous. Yet also he is powerful and responsible, even in his enchantment. It's the ones who, like Bluebeard, are a little bit too charming on the outside that we should be extremely wary of. What is so scary is that such characters demonstrate a truth about our collective human nature. We all have split-off parts which have somehow become divorced from the whole, parts that seek power in the knowledge that to do so is to go against self, against humanity and against God.

The brothers in this tale are able to differentiate. They understand precisely what they are dealing with in the figure of Bluebeard, and they act without hesitation. The vultures will eat his remains.

The brothers represent the blessing of strength and action. With them in the end, several things occur: one is that the vast and disabling ability of the predator is neutralised in a woman's psyche. And second, the blueberry-eyed maiden (however old she is) is replaced by one with eyes awake. And third, a warrior to each side of her if she will but call for them.[48]

In the Tarot, Death is the card of transformation. Those characters who, like Bluebeard, are killed off in myth and fairytale often portray aspects of the self that cannot be transformed in any other way. They must be stopped in their tracks, rendered to their essence and given a new start in another form, another life, call it what you will.

48   Estes, ibid, p. 58

We need 'vultures' in the psyche, says Estes, just as much as we need 'the sisters,' 'the brothers' and the quick wit of the young girl, gained through harsh experience. Vultures in fairytales have a magical role to play, for they consume, and in so doing recycle the scraps that are left over when the battle is done, the bits that no other animal can stomach. So ultimately nothing is left undone and even the dark heart of the predator (the fallen angel, if you like) has the possibility of transformation. It is a role that is vital in the process of transformation, for in eating what is left over, we literally digest evil, take it into ourselves, break it down and, most crucially, take from it such qualities as cunning, alertness, the ability to track, to sniff and smell our way through reality. Then we know instinctively who is who and what is what and use this information for the benefit of our souls; not in order to entrap or disempower others, but to set ourselves free, to empower and to render ourselves safe and secure in our worlds.

The rest, that which is anti-life, anti-love, anti-humanity, is returned into the bowels of the earth.

So, how does the combined action of the newly-awakened girl, the sisters, the brothers and the vultures translate into everyday terms? And how do we know when the job has been done, or is at least in process? We find that we are no longer susceptible to predatory charms. As a result, we begin to attract new experiences into our lives: wholesome ones, not the same pattern repeating itself *ad infinitum*. This is because we have learned new steps in the dance, steps that involve re-honouring ourselves, our deep, soulful aspirations and, crucially, our power to differentiate, to keep safe. We are no longer so dangerously naïve.

All along, it seems as though *boundary issues* were part of the problem. Paradoxically, they are part of the solution too; the trick is knowing where to place them, understanding precisely what they are intending to keep at bay and learning to deploy them appropriately. We understand now that by default, through naïvety, we created a chink, an open door, through which the predator stepped and laid us low.

Now we know better. We are in possession of a treasured new alertness and have rediscovered an 'ancient' psychic muscle with which to protect those aspects of our lives that bring meaning and joy: fierce, warrior-like qualities with which to defend the values and the people, including ourselves, that we love the most.

And, most amazingly, all this without closing our hearts.

The object is not to become hard; just more intelligent, more aware.

Lessons such as these, learned the hard way, become treasures, even though we may have scars to bear as an everlasting reminder of what we have lived through and survived.

But before we move on, we have a difficult job in front of us. For in order to proceed cleanly, we must also acknowledge the role that the predatory force has played in our story. Before we send him finally on his way to another time, another place, another less destructive form, he too must be recognised as part of the whole.

To honour the role that 'evil' has played in our lives is the hardest job of all, the hardest part of the story to deal with. Yet but for its appearance, there would have been no opportunity to evolve as we have done.

And in the end we have to recognise this. Like the serpent that tempted the innocent from paradise; like Zeus, who sanctioned the abduction of Persephone; and even like the evil Kings who raped the muses of the Holy Grail and caused the land to be laid waste, the predator, though it is not his intention, fulfils a divine function. To be innocent and to fall is part of being human, part of our universal story. The crucial thing is how we pick ourselves up, dust ourselves down and find our way back home. To arrive there we must grapple with hard truths, truths that we wish were not so. But, in the end,

it is up to us whether we overcome the negative aspects of the quest within ourselves, the anti-grail kings and their servants, and have in the end the satisfaction of seeing the dual aspects of the search united in one – the ultimate mystery of the Grail.[49]

---

49   John Matthews 1978, p. 100

Persephone's Secret

Hail, hail and thrice hail Persephone,
Queen of the night.
Into your embrace shall we commend our souls at death.
For truly you will bring us home.

Our story began with a secret, and in their own ways all of the stories considered have shed light upon the issue of secrets, each illuminating the matter from slightly different angles. There is a secret, too, at the heart of the Elusinian mystery initiations: what became of Persephone in the underworld?

For a long time this secret evaded me. There were many ways in which I had come to terms; many, many ways in which I had let go. Yet still there was a sense of incomprehension, still a veil obscuring the nature of what had happened on the level of the soul. Then, all at once, the myth disclosed something I had not seen before. It concerned the ingestion of the pomegranate seeds that had been given to Persephone by Hades, who had abducted her. What did it mean to eat them?

Now, from our position on the earth we may say that
when the visible surface of the moon is dark, Persephone
and all she represents is lost. This indeed is one level of the
mystery and, in the Elusinian Initiations, this gut-wrenching
loss was mourned for many days and nights, as is right and
proper in the face of such tragedy.

Yet mysteries by their nature are many-layered. The
deeper our perception, the deeper the truth revealed. Like
the initiates before us, we must return again and again to the
contemplation of these things, if we too are to partake of the
seed of transformation at their core. There is a *greater
mystery* at hand, a paradox of light and dark that threatens
to scramble our minds completely. Yet we must incorporate
it if we can, for it reveals a hidden truth. It is one that seems
impossible to bear, most especially where there has been
tragedy, but it is truth nevertheless.

In order to illumine this mystery we must look into the
meaning of these seeds. Now, when the moon is dark she is
nonetheless in relation with the sun, whose light floods her
far surface, whilst from the earth she cannot be seen at all.
In terms of the lunation cycle, it is said of this time that the
moon is seeded by the sun. The feminine soul is archetypally
associated with the moon, as the sun is with the spirit. God
is of the sun, of the day and of conscious life, whereas the
goddesses are by their nature in and of the moon, of the
night, of our unconscious life.

Together, sun, moon and all they have come to represent
form an exquisite whole, a unity and atonement mirrored as
a Sacred Marriage in the mythological and spiritual
outpourings of humankind. This sacred marriage, this
fusion of the feminine soul and the masculine spirit, is a
symbol of the wholeness within the self. It is the inner goal

of the Lunar Voyage, in which earth, sun and moon are momentarily aligned as the moon completes her wanderings through the sky and meets her solar bridegroom. It is then that she receives his seed, so that life may come again.

This image of sexual love is truly sacred, a sacrament at the deepest and most private core of the marriage celebration. For at this time it is said that the goddess of the moon has found her mate, the god of the sun. And when this happens there is cause for great celebration and the peoples of the earth rejoice and give thanks, for what was lost is now found.

Sexual love is potentially the most creative of acts but, robbed of its sacred dimension, it may also be the focus of the most destructive acts.[50]

For if the feminine soul is seized against her will – if what is precious is taken, rather than given – the moon, metaphorically speaking, is said to disappear. She flees away into the darkness, and no one knows if she will ever return. The ultimate goal of these cycles of transformation is to be united with our true sun, with our own spirit; but first we must uncover what has become of the moon.

Rape and sacred marriage are two sides of the same story. Both occur when the moon is dark; but whereas the divine coupling renews the world and its peoples, the profane brings both the land and human folk to their knees. In the former constellation, the sacred marriage is shrouded in mystery and hidden from mortal eyes. The moon bathes in solar light. Nothing can be seen from the earth. In the latter constellation, there is also shrouding and secrecy, but it does not enhance sanctity. Rather, it conceals a desecration in which the needs of the whole are for a while completely overturned. Yet there is hope, as the stories eventually

---

50   Caitlin Matthews 1991, p. 54

reveal. Then it will be said of us too that what was lost has been found and, like the ancients before us, there will be cause for great celebration.

It is undeniable that soul evolves from innocence to experience through some of the most harrowing realms of human life; and all rites of passage, ancient and modern alike, involve a similar sequence. The child is abruptly separated from her parents and initiated into a deep and terrifying truth, from which she will emerge changed. This is one aspect of the dark moon, this sudden abduction from the known and innocent life, this encounter with a darkness from which our cries may not be heard, where what happens is so terrifying that a part of the self in fact dies. This is the terrible tomb in which innocence is irretrievably lost. What happens here is sometimes called 'the initiatory wound' from which recovery is often long and far from certain.

Yet the mystery hinted at throughout is that the 'tomb' of the dark moon is also a 'womb' from which the self may be reborn. For, in dying to her past, Persephone attains a new maturity; and in eating the pomegranate seeds and integrating their hidden and secret knowledge into herself, she eventually becomes Queen of the Underworld.

Hail, hail and thrice hail Persephone,
Queen of the night.
Into your embrace shall we commend our souls at death.
For truly you will bring us home.

It is not for no reason that she is hailed in this way.

It is not for no reason, in her role below the earth, that thereafter she embraces the souls of the dead at the moment of death.

It is not for no reason that it is she, now knowing the perilous terrain by heart, who leads those lost souls through the underworld toward their own rebirth. For she has seen beyond the veil and incorporated the seed at the core of the mystery.

It is precisely through ingesting the pomegranate seeds, through taking them into herself, transforming them into sustenance rather than damage to her soul, that this wisdom, this precious fruit, has come about. Persephone becomes what is known as the *wounded healer*. It is through her terrible wound, inflicted during the dark phase of the moon, that she has attained the progressed state of being through which she is enabled to serve all who come after her. And, in the end, this most perilously acquired consciousness will lead her, and those who follow, to the heart of this mystery.

More than anything else, the myth of Demeter and Persephone speaks to us of an ever-renewing and unbroken circle. Its contemplation offers profound insight into the cycle of loss, search and recovery. The myth of the moon goddess tells that she gave birth to the universe out of herself, that she was the source of all life, the vessel of creation through which the cycle turned ever onward and life was continually renewed. The crops flourished and withered in their season, as did mortals, born out of her body, rising like the corn and being cut down at death. This is the face of the goddess as Demeter, as mother of the world, of life.

Yet at the moment of death she was there too, waiting to embrace her children, as she was there to embrace the sun at the end of each day, scooping it up into her deepest depths, into her womb. And from what she collected at death's dark door – the seed, as it were – she created new life each morning, each season, giving birth anew. This role

of guardian of the soul through death is the face of the
goddess as Persephone, Queen of the Underworld. You see,
in the end Demeter and Persephone are one, each giving
form and poetic expression to two very different yet
complementary aspects of the goddess of the moon. In
ancient Greece, as we have seen,

> Demeter and Persephone were the subject of a mystic
> drama as Eleusis celebrated with torches the abduction
> of the daughter and the sorrowful wanderings of the
> mother.

And of those who witnessed its annual enactment it is said,

> Blessed is she who has seen this and thus goes beneath the
> earth; she knows the end of life, she knows the beginning,
> for enacting Demeter's search and identifying with
> Persephone is precisely to wander in the underworld of
> death, just as the finding of Persephone is a return from
> death to life.[51]

---

51   Baring & Cashford, ibid, p. 381

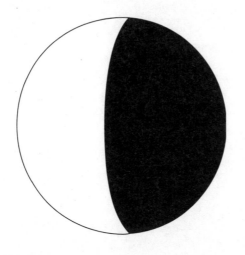

the waning quarter moon

steps towards forgiveness

Steps towards Forgiveness

'Thank you for breaking my heart,
thank you for tearing me apart.
Now I've a strong, strong, heart,
thank you for breaking my heart.' [52]

I write about my journey in linear terms. This is an illusion. Like the moon it waxes and wanes in an eternal round of light and darkness, of knowing and not knowing, of forgiving and not forgiving and all that this implies. We do not arrive once and for all at the condition of the new moon, so to speak. Forgiveness has many cycles, many phases. However, the hard truth is that *when an injury is done to us, we never recover until we forgive.* [53] But it is not easy.

Forgiveness is complex and often painfully hard; if it were not it would have no power to be life-changing. [54]

It was months before I could even begin to write this chapter. Although I had a file open on my computer from the outset, for a long time it was an empty file. Sometimes it was a confused file. I didn't even know if it should be there at all. I resented the part of me that knew that sooner

---

52 *Thank You For Hearing Me* Words and Music by Sinéad O'Connor and John Reynolds
53 Alan Paton in Mayne 2001, p. 172
54 Mayne, ibid. p. 167

or later I would have to let it go, let it be. My first attempts were not heartfelt. I was blocked and relied far too heavily upon the wise ideas of others that I failed to make my own. I longed for the moment when I would sit down and deliver, but it didn't happen, not for a long time. There was too much bitterness inside me. There comes a time, usually in mid-life, writes Clarissa Pincola Estes,

> *... when a woman has to make a decision – possibly the most important psychic decision of her future life – and that is, whether to be bitter or not ...*

All her dreams may be in ruins, her sacred lands invaded, burnt and razed to the ground.

> *But if a woman will return to the instinctual nature instead of sinking into bitterness, she will be revivified, reborn.*[55]

This was the light at the end of the tunnel, the little house of hope seen from the distance, smoke from the chimney, food in the pot, a warm fire in the grate and the welcome of ages at the open door. Oh, but sometimes it seemed so very far away! Surely it was just a dream and didn't exist at all?

The stages on this arduous journey are unique to each individual. For me it has felt important to tell my story, to make sense of where I have come from and where I am going. It's important, too, that our stories be heard. This in part is the point of the telling: to be heard. The hearing sets us free. For when finally we are understood, when our difficult feelings find their place in the story, we automatically relax and let go.

---

55   Estes, ibid. p. 364

Telling and being heard are pivotal steps in this challenging dance of forgiveness. Both were integral to the groundbreaking Truth and Reconciliation Commission which first practised in South Africa. This innovative approach to the healing process, though still profoundly limited, represented a huge step forward for humanity. It snapped a long historical chain by overturning all established precedents and challenging the root assumptions of past conflict management. Its adoption was transformative, for it offered people *the chance to be heard by those who had hurt them.*[56]

The sharing of stories creates empathy, the second step in the dance of forgiveness. Empathy causes the gap to close up between differing perspectives, different realities, so that we may be set free from besmirching the other. Through empathy we are enabled to withdraw our projections and in so doing open our hearts and minds to another's predicament, another's pain. This enables us to begin to make sense of their actions, for 'the other' invariably gives expression to part of the story, part of the truth that has been missing. Putting it all together creates a much bigger story, a much bigger truth, a much more intricate dance in which it becomes increasingly difficult to see absolute rights or wrongs.

When I put myself in the shoes of those who deceived us, it is easy to see the dilemmas they faced: the impossibility of finding a win/win scenario, a single 'right' to hold onto. With empathy I can see all these things. I can imagine all the painful stories, stories that by their nature will be very different from my own.

Even the perpetrator has his story. It does not excuse him, of course, but at least it goes some way towards

---

56   Mayne, ibid. p. 174

explaining his actions. His is a tale of terrible and sustained abuse that he himself suffered throughout childhood at the hands of a family member.

There are many stories yet to emerge, often with meanings still trapped between the lines, including this one. But no doubt everyone involved has been catapulted onto their own unique journey as a result of parts played. Who knows what has been learned as a result. But one thing is sure: everyone will be changed.

Time has now passed, my feelings have lessened in their intensity and I can see it all from new and previously obscured angles which can honour those who kept the secret. And the most important person I want to honour is my daughter, who not only survived her ordeal but went out of her way to protect us from the pain of it all.

It's difficult to imagine what we would do in a similar situation; it's very likely that the majority of us would have at least considered acting in this way. For there is a very real sense in which, by keeping things to ourselves, things that would inevitably rock relationships to their roots, we are enabled to preserve a degree of sanctuary from our own pain and from that of others: pain that very often may be more than we or they can bear. *'Whilst ever you were in the dark,'* she eventually told us, *'life could continue as normal. The house was my sanctuary. The fact that you didn't know was the only thing that kept me sane.'*

Her words reveal a truth about the protective role of secrets, of confidentiality. The tragedy of secrets, as we have seen, is the very great cost to the self of keeping them. For a long time it was incredibly difficult for us to appreciate her loving intention towards us. We fell into a kind of myopia in which all we could see was the cost. But it feels tremendously important that we acknowledge these intentions now. Why? Because otherwise we miss out on the reality of this love, this courageous attempt not to cause us pain, this intelligent calculation that in truth we would not be able to bear it. Recognising all this goes a long way towards tempering our experience, because we are now in a position to feel this love; and when we feel loved, so much of the distance between us just melts away.

Those who shared our daughter's confidence cared for us too, I am certain, and had no intention to hurt or cause us harm. This is not to say that we were not betrayed, that we did not suffer grievously in the wake of choices made; but that we have reached an understanding, through time, through empathy, through putting ourselves in others' shoes. And in this sense we can move more easily toward forgiveness.

Empathy is part of remembrance, the third step in the dance of forgiveness. To forgive and forget is not a viable option. We will never forget. And in any event to forget is to *dis*-member the sacred whole. To *re*-member is to bring the severed parts back together. Remembering leads more organically towards forgiving than forgetting ever can.

When the Egyptian god Osiris was murdered by his jealous brother, and his body dismembered into fourteen parts and scattered across the length and breadth of Egypt, his wife and sister, the twin goddesses Isis and Nepethys, could not rest nor could new life come again until they had gathered all the parts together and 're-membered' them as was fitting.

And wherever a part was discovered, a great temple was erected, so that their story might never be forgotten. But deep in the south of the country, on a small island in the Nile, the most beautiful temple of all was raised up, for it was here that they discovered the heart of Osiris, and it was here too that, through their magic arts, Isis and Nepythys re-membered him and made him whole.

With their great shimmering wings they breathed life back into their beloved, his heart quickened and stirred and the bright blood of youth coursed once more through his veins.

Nine months later, Isis gave birth to a beautiful, healthy son – a new cycle had begun.

To arrive at this place, this new beginning, is the goal of the sorrowful wanderings of all the goddesses of the moon. It is why they search, why they gather and collect the fragments of the whole together, so that they may be revivified and made whole; so that life may come again.

Again: re-membrance engenders forgiveness more than forgetting ever can. We cannot live fully with a festering wound, however we push it aside. This is a kind of repressive forgetting which leads only to more trouble. The way of remembrance, on the other hand, can release and transform old pain so that ultimately we are set free. Then we may forget in a more wholesome way. It is done; we are flushed clean and we can move into the future with as little debris as possible.

Through reconnection with the heart, compassion is engendered, the fourth step in the dance. Compassion is a quality of being rather than doing, a quality, a gentle light within which empathy and remembrance can be approached. Without it, all our efforts will be in vain.

And lastly (but in reality there is no order in these matters) we must acknowledge the importance of reflection upon our own part in the story. When I focus my attention here now, from a distance of nearly three years, it is clear that in my agony I ended up by becoming very self-righteous toward those who would not hear my point of view. I became evangelical and full of moral high ground, the very things I detested so much in others. Yet now I see that what I encountered in these people was actually a mirror of this part of myself. In this sense I unconsciously contributed to the deadlock that resulted between family and friends and caused much misery besides.

To look into this mirror is part of forgiveness, part of the mysterious dance of recovery; for when we see ourselves reflected in the difficult behaviour of others we can finally begin to unravel the complexity of what has transpired between us.

As I write, some of us are still estranged, either completely or partially, unable or afraid to reach out to one another and lay our ghosts to rest. Loss of trust is at the root of it; hurt embedded like shrapnel in wounds, so deep that some cannot even find a voice. And if they could, even if they can, they have little trust that this voice could ever be sympathetically heard. The task ahead must surely now turn toward creating the gentle conditions in which those who have yet to come forward feel safe to do so.

Now, as the moon wanes towards its last quarter, it can look like a great huge soup ladle emptying its contents into the sky. The moon is completing its progression toward a new cycle. In an astrological context this is seen as a time of releasing. In nature, this phase of the waning moon corresponds symbolically with autumn. Afterwards the land will lie fallow for a while, turned in on itself, gestating the seed of what has been constellated in the previous cycle. In time, new shoots will appear and raise their heads above the earth. Such shoots herald new beginnings in the unfolding story of our lives.

Forgiveness belongs to and is part of the harvest at the end of the cycle. In the garden the trees shed their fruit, which is ripe and ready to be picked. It is a time of abundance, of generosity, a time of letting go. How we finally arrive here, or how long will be our journey to this place, this season, this phase of the cycle within ourselves, none of us know. But, one day – 'Hey – here we are, standing under a harvest moon, picking the fruit of forgiveness from our own tree.'

What was seeded at the time of the dark moon now bears fruit. Telling our story, being heard, empathy, compassion – remembrance and reflection upon our part – each releases us, little by little lightening the heavy load of our suffering until in the end it simply dissolves. Deep down we know when we have arrived here. The debilitating adrenaline of rage ceases to pump through our bodies; we are no longer consumed by unresolved questions, irrespective of whether we have answered them or not. We have found a way to live. As a result, we begin to sleep more peacefully and wake rested in the mornings. Trust returns and our attention gradually re-focuses on the positive parts of our lives, the life in front of us. The past slips into the background; finally we are moving on.

Around about this time we had a bonfire. My husband set out lights and candles and brought his pot-bellied stove to the centre of our garden. Then there was a knock at the door.

A few days earlier I'd had a text message from a friend with whom I'd broken contact during the year. Amongst my close friends, she was probably the one who had helped our daughter the most, and in so doing had helped us. We have been through thick and thin over the years and have worked together creatively as well as being friends. She is the most wonderful pianist. 'How are you?' she wrote, rather tentatively. We had fallen out, you see. Big time! She had taken the full thrust of my anger. On the morning of the bonfire I had replied, 'I miss you'. She was the perfect person to arrive that night. We hugged and smiled and talked all at once. Later we went outside to watch the fire and warm ourselves through by it.

The sting had gone out of what had happened between us. She knew where I had been coming from all along. She had anticipated a whole range of reactions that I might have; she had said to me earlier in the year that she knew she stood to lose either my or my daughter's friendship, possibly even both, as a result. When the hard part came, as inevitably it did, we just needed a little time away from each other to let things settle, as we both knew they would. After a while we came out on the other side, our relationship stronger as a result. We went through it, you see; we talked until there was nothing left to say, until we understood and loved each other again. Then we were free to watch and warm ourselves by the fire, without speaking a word.

We have strayed far, far from heaven on this journey to atonement. We have all of us fallen into deep shadow. Yet beyond this bleak terrain, this wasteland through which we have passed, there is yet another place, another realm or phase if you like, another state of being. Closer to heaven by far than those shadowy recesses of the soul, the like of which were shown to Dante *en route* to Paradise. But not quite heaven yet. And what we see here, eventually, is an abrupt inversion of the previous truth, in which the players re-configure to reveal an opposite and hitherto undreamt-of reality. For here in this more light-filled realm it turns out that in fact, contrary to all our beliefs, our enemies turn out to be our greatest helpers. For they show us the places *in ourselves* where we were most disconnected from the light.

And behind this and deeper still, or yet higher or nearer the centre, is another even more radiant realm that the poets have called Heaven or Paradise, Avalon, Caer Siddi or the Honeyed Plain of Bliss. We arrive here, as we have seen, only when the moon is full; when there is no shadow to obscure the fullness of our souls. And here, finally, say those who have come back to us from this place, there is no drama at all; for here there are no opposites to play it out.

And should we ever chance upon this realm, should we succeed in our ultimate quest, then like the heroines and heros of myth and legend we too will be graced with the remembrance of all we have forgotton along the way. Then, instead of outrage at each other's actions, we will understand and find compassion, true and deep as never before. And we will see again as if through angel eyes. And in so doing, we will all be returned to innocence once more.

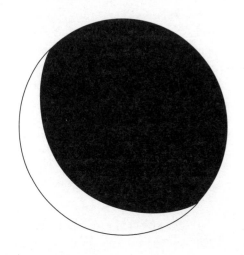

the balsamic moon

the return
only connect
the mystery of approach
the voyage of the Moon
back to Earth

The Return

I thought that my voyage had come to its end –
that the path before me was closed
But I find that thy will knows no end in me.
And when old words die out on the tongue,
new melodies break forth from the heart;
and where the old tracks are lost,
new country is revealed with its wonders.[57]

I have longed to gather the threads of resolution, and return to weave the endings of the myths and fairytales we have pondered and which have shed light on our personal predicament. At the start we were in despair; we had lost our way completely. 'To whom shall we turn?' we cried out in our anguish. 'Where are the maps? Who will guide us back home?'

When I shut and relaxed my eyes as a child I used to see a little luminous green circle. I called it 'the promise'. I still see it sometimes. The idea of promise gives hope. When Pandora's Box has sprung open and all the evils of the world have poured forth, hope alone remains. As Clarissa Pincola Estes counselled:

---

57 Gitanjali, in Tagore 1912, p. 29

The most important thing to do, *when your life is shattered and you have lost your way, is to hold on, hold out for your very life; for the promise from the wild nature is this: after winter, spring always comes.*[58]

Myths and fairytales can show us ways out of the darkness. They elucidate the process of recovery, of healing. They give us hope. For with the progression of each tale, the characters eventually configure in ways that bring about an alchemy of supreme transformation.

And so the hundred years of darkness drew to a close, and at that same time a young man of gentle nature stopped to rest at the cottage of a very old woman who had lived at the edge of the forest since she was a child. After she had fed him she began, as was the custom in her family, to tell the tale of the forest of thorn and the Sleeping Beauty who lay therein.

And as he listened to the old woman's tale, he understood at once that he was part of it, that in some strange way, the sleepers behind the hedge were his people and that the sleeping princess at the heart of it was his own future Queen. And he knew instantly and without doubt that he must find and awaken her. He ran outside and to his complete astonishment found that all the buds on the trees had burst into bloom and a pathway lay open before him.

At the centre of the palace gardens he came to the tower where the princess lay. At the very top, he arrived at the old arched door, as the girl had done before him. It was very dark in the little room beyond, but when his eyes had adjusted to the dim light, he saw a most beautiful sleeping girl. He knelt down beside her and kissed her sleeping face and, as he did so, she opened her eyes and smiled knowingly, as if she had been dreaming of him all along.

And at that same time, the spell cast at her christening party finally ran its course. The sun brightened in the skies and the forest of thorn vanished. At last the hundred years were done.

The awakening of the beautiful princess and the marriage that follows is a *motif par excellence* in fairytale, for it represents the reconciliation of opposites, of parts of the self – of the kingdom – that have by tragic circumstance become estranged from one another. This is the promise, the hope prefigured in the story: that one day these opposing tendencies will be reunited amidst great celebration. In the Moon Goddess mythology, in which all the tales we have considered have their ancient roots, this is the moment of the sacred marriage.

The soul awakens to the kiss of the prince who, as the solar bridegroom, consort of the moon goddess, personifies the divine masculine principle.[59]

He is the extreme opposite of Bluebeard; of the evil king who raped the muses of the sacred well; of the dark lord of Hades into which Persephone was stolen; of the spindle that inflicted the wound on the young princess. Indeed he is the opposite of anyone who consciously degrades another. He is full-blooded and warm. He is strong where the old king was weak, he is wise in a way that the old king was not, and because of this wisdom he will be able to protect his queen from danger in a way that the old king could never do.

59   Baring & Cashford, ibid. p. 681

His arrival heralds a completely new order, an evolutionary progression of consciousness that brings a healing so profound that the past is completely overturned. We might ask why and how this can be so. The answer is simply that he puts the princess back in touch with the part of herself, the 'living rose' at the centre of her soul, that has lain behind the thorny wood for so long. For the truth is that she has been cut off from herself every bit as much as she has been from the world beyond.

Yet see how easily this hero is allowed to proceed, where so many have failed before. See how the princess seems to sense his arrival. For the parting trees surely suggest that the grip on some long-defended parts of herself is being loosened; now she dares to trust once more.

To my mind this is the most poignant scene of the fairy-tale; the one for which, were I to put it on as a play, I would save my very best musical score. And if I were making a film, I would slow it right down; the entire approach as seen through the eyes of the prince, from the very first stirring of the branch as it bent upon its bough, to the exquisite unfolding of every bud and the blooming of each colourful flower. For this parting of trees and magical re-appearance of spring is truly an image of a spell finally breaking. It is a clear invitation from the hitherto sleeping princess to the approach of her beloved.

'*I slept*,' sang Solomon's bride, in one of the most poetic renderings of the sacred marriage texts to have been preserved from ancient times.

I slept, but my heart is awakened.
Listen; it is the voice of my beloved calling:

'Rise up, my love, my fair one, and come away.
For, lo, the winter is past, and the rain is over and gone;
The flowers appear on the earth; the time of the singing
of birds is come, and the voice of the turtle dove is heard
in our land.' [60]

This mystical image restores to the psyche the longed-for experience of wholeness, of oneness in the self and in our relations with 'the other' and also the divine. It is the highest ideal and ultimate goal of the soul, and thus represents the attainment and completion of the lunar quest. Sadly, the collective and personal loss of this sacred image in which all things are most mercifully reconciled *'has inflicted a deep wound on the soul, which has yet to be healed.'* [61]

One hundred years is a long time to be so lost. At such times patience is indeed a virtue for, in a very real way, time and nature eventually put a distance between us and the raw extremes of our pain; but if we want healing we must also be prepared to tackle the inner questions.

For when the feminine, feeling side of life is in retreat,
'life is nothing but thorns for one hundred years'. [62]

Now, as we have seen, the outcome of Sir Percival's quest turns upon his ability to ask a crucial question. In a sense the entire quest is his question, for to quest is to question. Our questions unlock the truth, about ourselves as well as others, and ultimately bring about the action of the Grail. But first he must face a final challenge:

Well, eventually, the path to the lost Court of Joy was revealed and our hero made haste, full of faith – at last home was within sight.

---

60   Song of Solomon 2: 10-12
61   Bashing & Cashford, ibid. p. 657
62   Chetwynd, ibid. p. 377

Then suddenly and without warning, the path ahead cracked open and plunged into a deep and terrible abyss. Oh, and the mournful cries of many lost souls rose up in despair from below.

Our hero reeled, his spirits plunged and the castle ahead began most inauspiciously to spin.

This is a critical hurdle for Sir Percival. His faith in the realisations wrought from the quest are now tested to the hilt.

Dealing with any major life-crisis, we tend to take one step forward and two back; it's just how it goes. Points along the way are visited not only once but many, many times until the healing is done. It often seems that, as soon as we grasp a truth, the universe tests us, both to make sure we've got the message and to give us an opportunity to process more of our stuff if we need to. Easy to grasp with our minds; not so easy when we are dragged back toward the nightmare.

If there is unfinished business (and, to be realistic, there usually is), this is where we struggle. If we still have work to do, flashbacks of the nightmare may return to haunt us. If this keeps happening, we may need to seek help. Those who have worked in the field of trauma counselling will recognise in the motif of the cracked and plunging path a complexity of the healing process. There are flashbacks, setbacks. Despite all our best efforts, the nightmare can come suddenly and unexpectedly back to life and threaten to devour us all over again. Who knows how long we may linger upon the edge of this abyss? Who knows how long it will be before the terror is fully passed and we are free to proceed?

The process of recovery is a delicate and often lengthy business, as we have seen, but it is possible. In the end we, like Sir Percival, will be free to move on. To realise the challenge of the moment of greatest doubt, we must transform it into a moment of greatest faith; and we *must* proceed. Reassuringly, Sir Percival is not found wanting but, strengthened in his resolve, chooses not to give in to his fate; he rather leaps forward in the fullness of faith, finally to claim his destiny.

Now, no one knows exactly how he proceeded from this place. Some say it was by way of a perilously narrow bridge that appeared then before him. But others proclaim that, magically, the great golden wings embroidered on his cloak quickened and stirred to life and Sir Percival was at once borne upwards and onwards to the spinning castle ahead.

And there a place was already prepared for him at a great round table, where sat the keepers and the seekers of the Grail from all the centuries of the quest. And each one present had a story to impart. Then the rich fisherman, who presided at that place, led the young Sir Percival, with the knights of his own time, to a small chapel where still the wounded King cried out in his torment. And there Sir Percival witnessed again the mysterious procession of the Holy Grail.

And when finally he asked, 'Whom does the Grail serve?' he immediately understood that he should offer it to the wounded and long-suffering King. And as he placed the Holy Vessel to the parched lips of that man he was at once completely healed, the castle ceased to spin and the waste lands burst forth into a glorious flowering of spring.

In the annual re-enactment of the Demeter and Persephone mystery, the ancient priestesses of Eleusis processed toward the inner sanctum of their temples, mirroring the path of Demeter, resting and reflecting as she rested and reflected along the way. The third and final place of transition was called The Laughless Rock. Beyond was the Bridge of Jests, which gave access to the sacred ground of renewal ahead. Transposed onto the lunar cycle (and this time corresponds to the time of the last quarter moon), it is a phase of deepening re-orientation. It is here that something very unexpected occurs.

Now, it is often extremely difficult to know how to be around people who are in distress. But sometimes, as Clarissa Pinkola Estes prescribes, a little bit of humour can be just the right medicine to tip the scales into a more favourable position. So it was in the myth.

Well, neither deathless god nor mortal man could raise Demeter from her sorrow, until finally a little dancing girl came before her as she rested by the Laughless Rock. No one else dared come near – but this little dancing girl – who was in truth a sister spirit come in disguise to assist her – approached quite playfully and made her laugh.

Humour breaks the mood, loosens the grip of our sadness, cracks a hole in the darkness and allows the light to come streaming through, if only for a second. But sometimes a second is all we require, to step back in the sudden realisation that enough is enough. Yet it can't be just anybody who comes along and cracks a joke, it's got to be done with immense precision and timing, as any good comedian will know. However, the little dancing girl knows just when to make her move: what to do and how to make the goddess smile.

In other versions of the story, the dancing female is portrayed as Baubo, a voluptuous serving maid. She approaches Demeter as a woman of the world, wriggling her hips, shaking her skirts, flirting outrageously, telling secret woman's jokes: reminding Demeter of the joys of the flesh and diverting her attention away from its perils. [63]

Such wholesome and shameless sensuality transforms the Laughless Rock into the Rock of Laughter's Return and in so doing creates a psychic bridge, giving access to the holy ground of renewal ahead.

This inner sanctum is not only a literal place in the temple. It's also a place within: the core of the dance around which all our sorrowful wanderings revolve. When Demeter finally laughs, she does not literally get up and cross the Bridge of Jests. No. What happens is that the laughter lights her up and, when she is lit from within, winter at last begins its transition into spring. The little dancing girl and the voluptuous Baubu have moved the story on.

And on the other side of the moon – in the underworld, so to speak – it is as if Persephone is waiting for all this is to occur; as if she cannot possibly return above until her mother recovers her ability to laugh. Like the myth of the Holy Grail, that of Demeter resolves with the rebirth of spring and the triumphant return of Persephone from the underworld. At last the gods relent, a compromise is reached, Demeter's trust is renewed and she ceases to withhold. Spring returns and with it her beautiful daughter. Finally the two are re-united.

---

63   See Estes, p. 338 & Hall, p. 82

But only for two thirds of the year. Things cannot be returned to exactly where they were, otherwise there would have been no point, no rhyme or reason to their story. Nothing is the same. The past is gone. Our daughter, like the daughter of Demeter, is grown into a young woman. The separation, which is a true goal of adolescence, has been achieved. Persephone is now a fully-fledged goddess in her own right and not primarily in relation to her mother. In psychological terms, she has achieved a new maturity.

Mythologically, her name will forever be associated with the rebirth of spring. The long winter of transition has been painful, as parents the world over know only too well; but in the end we, like Demeter, must accept this basic fact, this ever-changing, never-ending cycle of life.

It is salutary to consider that birds who do not fly the nest, those who lack the courage to wrest themselves free of parental clutches however warm and comforting, do not in the end achieve the same levels of individuation as their flyaway counterparts. Though the earth may rock as they defiantly hold out for their autonomy and their own definitions of themselves, the promise of maturity heralds new life for all concerned.

Now, as we have seen, there is a sense in which, when Demeter searches for her lost child, she is also searching for a lost part of herself, that which her daughter represents. Maybe part of her needs to get lost; maybe she too has to experience a further initiatory wound, a new shattering of innocence that causes her in the end to become yet more aligned with her soul.

And what of Persephone? What finally can we say of her; of our own lovely daughter? That she has suffered greatly is without doubt. That she bears the scars of all who have experienced the terrors of the underworld? Certainly! What happens behind the scenes, beyond the ever-watchful gaze of parents, creates (if it does not kill us) a consciousness of the sort that brings membership of a particular clan: the 'scar clan', as Estes calls it. You don't have to be any particular age to join, you just have to have lived through something very, very big, and survived.

The scars will always be with us, parents and children alike; yet in time we will come to cherish them, hard as it may seem. For they will *remind* us, as the stories do, and make us stronger. They will be like markers on our path that show the routes we have taken, and give us clues as to how to proceed toward the light, toward the sacred, toward even greater healing. [64]

The legends are greater than we are. This is for sure; but if they had nothing to say to us personally, if they did not resonate, fascinate, they would not have survived the transition through the centuries. Their ultimate meaning we can but ponder, but we should never forget that there is so much more to them than meets the eye. They are full to the brim and as potent and highly distilled as a full-bodied wine.

The writing of this book has sustained me. It started with an idea and a small circular diagram depicting the cycle of the moon, onto which I plotted the chapter titles, the phases of the journey ahead. We began in darkness, a shadow completely obscuring our lives: the phase of the Dark Moon. As time passed, we progressed. Gradually the shadow lifted and little by little, from the first appearance of the crescent through to the waxing of the first quarter and half moon, our predicament became more clear. The shadow was

64   See Estes 1992, 'Battle Scars: Membership in the Scar Clan'

lifting, and it continued to lift through the second quarter and on to the full.

This is where we saw clearly the revelation of where we were; of what had been constellated or seeded at the beginning of the cycle. And as the moon waned, returning as it must into the darkness, we reflected upon all that had been revealed. The feminine light of the moon, of the soul, did not desert us, even though there were times along the way when her light seemed totally obscured. She was there nevertheless; her loss, like that of our daughter, merely an illusion.

Her return to us began in small ways; tiny, almost imperceptible changes, like snow slowly melting. After almost a whole year of keeping her distance, she was subtly changing around us. She joined us for coffee in the mornings, phoned to let us know if she was going to be late, started to say 'I love you' when she left the house. Little things; but, remember, there had been nothing for such a long time. We still could not go near 'the secret', but the desperation had gone out of us.

Our role has turned out to be very different from what we thought it would be, from what we wanted it to be. The mending of our fractured relationship is coming in much more subtle ways. Most importantly, we have had to step back and put our energies into creating a gentle, unthreatening environment in which we can all recover in our own time and in our own ways.

You know, I always thought that the end of this journey would be discovering the hidden world behind the secret: my daughter's story. But I find that this is not what it is about at all. It's about letting go of the past and *returning to myself.*

I would not have wished this journey on my worst enemy, nor would I have willingly chosen the complete meltdown and disintegration of what was. But we have all survived and in a very tangible sense we have been transformed. No doubt there will be new challenges, new obstacles, unfinished business and difficult voyages to undertake, but for the moment we have reached dry land; reached home.

There's a warm place inside. Glimmers of love and laughter have returned to our home.

I think it's going to be OK.

Only Connect

Only connect.... These famous words of E. M. Forster provide the focus for this chapter. At last we arrive at a place where we can begin to tie up some last loose ends, broaden our perspective and look back over the difficult terrain we have travelled, with the benefit of learning gained along the way. *'A person with "ubuntu"'*, writes Archbishop Desmond Tutu when describing the concept behind this unique African word, *'knows that he or she belongs in a greater whole'*.[65]

When one amongst us is diminished, we are as a whole diminished too. This recognition of the deep interconnectedness of life offers much, for it enables us to see that the violations experienced by individuals are part of and reflect something much wider.

The mythical wastelands of the Grail transposed into a contemporary setting are plain to see: Hiroshima, the unholy consequence of the edict 'divide and rule', the splitting of the atom, of science gone berserk, the furthest humanity has strayed from the centre of the dance, from unity and co-operation with nature, with the divine feminine.

---

65   Mayne, ibid. p. 174

Remember the dishonoured damsel in the Grail Quest who rebuked Sir Percival in the forest after he had failed to ask the question that would release the enchantments of Britain and heal the Wastelands? She was the damsel of *pure and matchless beauty*, who had once borne the Holy Grail itself; but it was *as if all the weight of time had come suddenly upon her*. She, like the Wounded King, like Demeter and Persephone, like the Sleeping Beauty, personifies and embodies the dual dimensions of the personal and the collective. They are one with the land, their destinies indivisible.

It is significant that the destruction of the earth through industrialisation and the relentless march of scientific reason divorced from spiritual and ecological ethics has occurred during an epoch when the feminine principle has been at best undervalued and at worst dishonoured. It has been said that what we do to the planet, we do to ourselves. To recognise this is to possess *ubuntu*.

Jules Casford and Anne Baring end their epic book *Myth of the Goddess* with a quotation from Chief Seattle who asks:

What will you teach your children? he asks. That the earth is our mother? What befalls the earth, befalls all the children of the earth. This we know: the earth does not belong to man, man belongs to the earth. All things are connected like the blood which unites us all. Man did not weave the web, he is merely a strand in it. Whatever he does to the web, he does to himself.[66]

Once upon a time, the notion of sacred space used to extend to the whole of creation, stretching outwards from the body of the earth and her children to the heavens

---

66   Baring & Cashford, ibid. p. 681

beyond, and inwards to the infinite recesses of the soul. Our task, the great work of our lives, is to remember this connectedness, this undeniable oneness of life; and in so doing to make sacred once more the sites of desecration both within ourselves and in the world we share. Much has been lost in the passage of time, including the natural wisdom of healing, of re-consecration. The ancient priestesses and wise women of antiquity possessed such gentle wisdom and employed it to great effect.

> *One of the greatest needs for healing, and one that is seldom recognised, is the aftermath of rape. The womb is the sacred centre of a woman and its violation is as great a desecration as that of a church ... but when a woman is raped, when the sacred centre where life is engendered ... when that is entered, torn, savaged and left unclean, what is offered to the woman?* [67]

Though as a culture we do our best, offering what love and professional support we can, the grim fact remains that the deep wounds of millions who have sustained such violation continue to bleed. But, Ashcroft continues, there is hope: hope that the flow of blood can be stemmed, *that the sacred place within her can be re-consecrated and her spirit made whole.* [68]

There are ways and there are ways. But if we understand that to be raped is to experience a trespass of the soul, we will understand also something of the depth of healing required. Whichever path you choose, I would say only: begin today.

The simplest things often seem hardest to achieve. Love yourself. Nurture, trust and have faith. Do not hide from

---

67   D. Ashcroft-Nowiki 1982, pp. 58-59
68   Ashcroft-Nowiki, ibid. p. 59

anything, shed light wherever you can, gather up your brokenness, do not be ashamed. Bring the severed parts to your own sacred place of healing, imaginary or real, and lay them down as treasures; whether they be painful memories or ones of joy, each are equally important. Gather as much as you can, ask questions, make a sense you can live with, honour all; the difficult bits especially. Celebrate the learning gained along your way.

Above all, be kind and generous to yourself. And whatever love you extend to others, remember always to give it to yourself as well. Then maybe, one day – one day soon, perhaps – you too will find a way home to the lost Court of Joy, the Grail of Transformation and Healing at the centre of your soul.

Our story is the stuff of myth. We have seen our struggles reflected here time and time again. But we have seen our return journey too, even glimpsed the vision and the promise of peace which is our ultimate destination. Such was the eventual reward of the brave and courageous souls who went in quest of The Holy Grail:

And when finally the Wastelands were healed, the knights of the Grail were spirited away to the high city of Sarras, where a final Mass of the Quest was celebrated midst a great company of angels. And at that time it was given unto them to bear the hallows of the Grail to the high altar of that place.

And she who preceded them all, and who bore the Holy Grail itself, was the once dishonoured damsel, now so restored that all who looked upon her imagined a glorious rising of the sun. Unto her it was given to offer up the Holy Vessel, unveiled at last to the heavens; whereupon a wondrous being of light appeared from within saying:

'My servants and my knights and my true children, who are come out of mortal life into spiritual life. Oh I will no longer hide from you but you shall see a part of my secrets and my hidden things. Now hold, and receive the high meat which you have so long desired.' [69]

---

69   Based on Thomas Malory, 'Le Mort D'Arthur', in Matthews and Green 1986, p. 54

The Mystery of Approach

In his beautiful book of Celtic spiritual wisdom, 'Anam Cara', John O'Donoghue explains: *anam* means 'soul' and *cara* is 'friend'. And if we are to befriend the soul of one who is very hurt, we must be mindful of our approach. We must come upon the mystery gently, reverently and indirectly, with candlelight, not electric light, to illumine our way.

The following fanciful stories were written on a cold winter's afternoon. I did not at all intend them for this book. I was working things through, seeing if I could find a new perspective from which to understand the distance between my daughter and myself. The stories came out quite whole, without my really thinking much as I wrote. This is the kind of dreamy writing I like best, because I know that when I read it back I might really learn something about myself. And I did.

The Girl with Three Mothers

Once upon a time there was a daughter with three Mothers. One night something terrible happened in the woods close to where they lived.

Well, the first mother, the youngest, collapsed into grief.

The second, a little older, flew into a rage.

But the third mother, the eldest, simply carried on as before. Yet in the evenings, when the sun hung low over the forest, she would light a candle in the window and ponder over the meaning of these things.

Now, the first and second mothers, though they did not intend it, drove their daughter away. For, you see, their sorrow and rage caused them to lose themselves and, in such a state of loss, they could do nothing to help their daughter. Whereas the third remained calm and a little detached, as was fitting.

Well, soon the lives of the first and second mothers fell apart, for their emotions were so overwhelming and so wearying that they quickly lost control of their affairs. They no longer knew the rhythm of day and night. For them all was night; all was dark. They could not eat, sleep, or indeed do anything required to create a bit of peace for their daughter, who was herself still attempting to recover from what had happened in the woods.

Now the trouble was that the poor girl never knew which of the mothers would be at home when she returned in the evenings. They kept on changing, you see.

When the first mother was at home, the young girl couldn't get any rest, for her nights were disturbed by her mother's constant sobbing.

It was no better when the second mother was at home, for she, it seemed, knew nothing at all about being a mother and would pace the floor from sunset till dawn, wringing her hands and muttering angrily to herself about everything that had gone on; which, as it happened, was the very thing the daughter couldn't bear.

Things were much better when the third mother was at home. There was food on the table, laughter in the air and each had restful nights at the end of the day.

Clearly the girl preferred the third mother and she showed her much appreciation. She couldn't talk about what had happened in the woods, so they talked about what they could, each knowing where the boundary had been set.

In these ways time passed.

During the day the daughter went about the business of her life. She did very well, but still it did not go easily for her when she returned to the house where the mothers were grieving and raging. And each evening as she made her way home, she longed to find the third mother waiting for her at the door.

Sometimes she was lucky.

More time passed. The girl's luck increased. For, you see, somehow it happened that the third mother was more and more at home and the others less and less.

Now one such evening much, much later, when the daughter sat together with the third mother, she decided to tell her about all the trouble she had had with the other two.

'Throughout the night,' she explained, 'one wept whilst the other raged. I could get no rest and was at my wits' end. Whatever was the matter?'

'Ah,' the elder mother sighed softly. 'I was wondering when you would ask.' She sat back in her chair to ease her back; for, you see, she was by now quite an old woman.

'To sense your wound,' she began at last, 'drove them practically insane, for it ripped open a place in them that was also wounded, a bleak, desolate place where every scrap of hope was turned to dust.'

The daughter did not reply at first but then said quite knowingly, 'Yes, I thought as much'.

Neither of them spoke for a long time.

But later the young woman said, 'One thing still puzzles me, though. I never did understand how some nights when I came home, I found *you* here, and not my weeping or raging mothers?'

'Oh,' replied the third mother, 'that's quite simple. For, you see, we three are really one and the same, but I am the part that got through.'

The Mother with Three Daughters

Once upon a time, there was a mother who had three daughters. One night something terrible happened in the woods close by.

Well the first daughter, the youngest, withdrew into a deep silence, whilst the second, a little older, became angry and defensive. But the third, the eldest of them all, simply carried on as before. Yet in the evenings, when the sun hung low over the forest, she would light a candle in the window and ponder over the meaning of these things.

Now the first and second daughters, though they did not intend it, drove the mother away; for, you see, their silence and defensiveness caused them to lose themselves and, in such a state of loss, they could do nothing to help their mother. Whereas the third remained calm and a little detached, as was fitting.

Well soon the lives of the first and second daughters fell apart, for their emotions were so overwhelming and so wearying that they quickly lost control of their affairs. They no longer knew the rhythm of the day. For them all was night; all was dark. They could not eat, sleep, or indeed do anything required to create a bit of peace for their mother, who was herself still attempting to recover from what had happened in the woods.

Now the trouble was that the poor mother never knew which of her daughters was coming home in the evenings. They kept on changing, you see. When the first daughter was at home, the mother could get no rest, for her nights were disturbed by the terrible silence.

It was no better when the second daughter was home. For she, it seemed, did not understand anything about being a daughter; she would stay out later and later and was even more defensive when she returned; which, as it happened, was the very thing the mother couldn't bear.

Things were much better when the third daughter was home. There was food on the table, laughter in the air; each had restful nights at the end of the day.

Clearly, the mother preferred the third daughter, and she showed her much appreciation. They couldn't talk about what had happened in the woods. So they talked about what they could, each knowing where the boundary had been set.

In these ways time passed.

During the day, the mother went about the business of her life. She did very well, but still things did not go easily for her when the silent and defensive daughters returned. And each evening as she waited at the door she longed to see the third daughter coming home.

Sometimes she was lucky.

More time passed. The mother's luck increased, for, you see, somehow it happened that the third daughter was more and more at home and the others less and less.

Now one such evening much, much later, as the mother sat together with her third daughter, she decided to tell her about all the trouble she had had with the other two.

'One was so silent and the other so defensive,' she explained. 'I was at my wits' end. Whatever was the matter?'

'Ah,' the third daughter sighed softly, 'I was wondering when you would ask.' Then she sat forward on her chair, for you see she was by now quite grown.

'To sense your wound,' she began at last, 'drove them practically insane, for it ripped open a place within them that was also wounded, a bleak, desolate place where every shred of hope had turned to dust.'

The mother did not reply at first but then said quite knowingly, 'Yes, I thought as much. But one thing still puzzles me. I never did understand how some nights when I was waiting at the door, I saw you and not my silent or defensive daughters coming home?'

'Oh,' replied the third daughter, 'that's quite simple. You see, we three are really one and the same, but I am the part that got through.'

The Voyage of the Moon

On this journey toward 'true home',
though we may, from time to time,
turn back to record or measure from whence we came,
we do not turn back in order to turn back.[70]

We enter the phase of the Dark Moon through loss. The past is snatched suddenly away and the new is totally unformed. The voyage of recovery is long, and those who embark, willing and unwilling alike, must first experience a world without form.

Many years ago I had a dream in which I left my home. I'd responded to a mysterious calling, a deep song that drew me down to a realm beneath the sea where I remained in darkness for what seemed like centuries. And in this dark, liquid realm, my human form dissolved and I became a fish, with scales and fins; then even this dissolved and I became a grain of sand, then a droplet of water.

But after a long time of proceeding in this way I became a grain of sand again, then a fish with scales and fins. And I heard once more the mysterious calling, the deep song that had drawn me. And as I listened I remembered my home

---

70   Estes, ibid. p. 478

and my loved ones far away; and remembering, I regained my human form and rose swiftly to the surface, eager for breath, for new life.

And there I saw the most beautiful crescent moon, floating as a magical boat of light toward me. And in this silvery vessel sat a very old, wizened woman, with long, plaited hair and strong, deeply weathered hands. She reached out toward me and hoisted me out of the water, into the boat beside her. I thought I knew her but wasn't sure, but I trusted her, for I knew she would take me home.

So together we set sail and on the way she sang to me and soothed me and told me stories of all the ancestors before. But however she sang, and there were many, many ways, one thing was always the same. Something precious was lost, searched for and finally found. And over the course of our long journey together, during which our silvery vessel changed shape many times, I came to understand that she was forever telling me the story of the soul, reflected in her ever-changing phases.

When finally I awoke, I fancied for a moment I was still lying in that boat. But then I found I was in the comfort of my own bed and that it had all been a dream. The old woman who had sung to me was gone, but I knew she had been there, for in my heart I could still recall her song. Clarissa Pinkola Estes might call her La Que Sabe, the old one who knows. Jung might have called her the two-million-year-old being, whose ancestry reaches back into the deepest layers of human experience.

There's a point, you see, where our individuality disappears and we are all one in a great sea of consciousness which is indivisible and shared. In our dreams we go there every night, like Alice stepping through the looking glass. And there we find a world quite unlike our own, a seemingly nonsense world where ridiculous and impossible things happen as a matter of course.

On some level, we all understand this peculiar realm with its peculiar poetic language that expresses things that can't be expressed in any other way. And, if we are to engage with the unconscious forces that have gripped our lives, we must learn this language, for within it the content of the unconscious finds its true voice.

There is much afoot at any given time that can make a shambles of spirit and soul by attempting to destroy intent, or by pressuring one to forget the important questions: questions such as, not only what are the pragmatics of a situation, but also, 'where is the soul in this matter?' [71]

At the start I thought I could answer this question by knocking on the doors of those who had supported my child. I thought they could tell me what had happened to her soul and why we had become estranged. I felt sure that one day she would speak to me herself and I would know. But for years this never happened. I was desolate and alone.

But now, all this time later, I see that I was not alone at all, that the arms of numerous helpers have reached out across space and time to embrace me, and that I have been soothed and sung to and told the stories of all the ancestors before. And together we have taken the Voyage of the Moon; we have seen the soul reflected in her ever-changing phases and slowly, very slowly, I have been returned to

71   Estes, ibid. p. 478

myself. Chances are that by the laws of synchronicity – and if you have read this far – the old one who knows, the two-million-year-old being, your own deep self, is reaching out to embrace you too.

Back to Earth

There's an old tradition in storytelling, a device if you like, designed to bring the listener and the teller back to earth, to ground and prepare us for ordinary life at the end of our voyage to other realms.

The self yearns to be lifted into the realms of the soul, to touch and be touched by that which is beyond; but while ever we live on this earth, we must know how to return here. The old storytellers kept it simple, saying, *and so they all lived happily to the end of their days and their story is kept safe in the realm of the soul; but as for us poor beggars, we're so hungry, after listening for so long, we're sucking on our teeth. So please, for the love of God, let's eat!*

Similar closing procedures are performed at the end of much religious ritual. The celebrant will often close the Catholic Mass, for example, by reading out everyday notices about the forthcoming week. Finally he says, 'The Mass is ended; go in peace.' The celebrants then depart, candles and lights are extinguished and normal life resumes.

For those of you who have followed the story of the Dark Moon, I would like to close with a few everyday notices of my own, just in case you were wondering....

The perpetrator was never arrested or charged, even though his actions were reported to the police, independently by myself and my daughter. We were both rejected as witnesses; my daughter because time had elapsed and there were no forensic evidence or witnesses; myself because all I had was 'hearsay'.

Shortly after the secret about our child came to light, my husband, step-daughter and myself devised a plan and successfully rescued others whom we surmised were at risk of violence. All our assumptions had been true. Six years later they have all made new lives.

As for my daughter, it is she who impresses me the most. To lose one's way when one is yet but a child, to become trapped within darkness, and to claw one's way back to the light is nothing short of a miracle. She is now more 'savvy' than you can imagine, as well as being one of the most loving and compassionate people I know.

And, last but not least, as a family we are closer now than we have ever been.

POSTSCRIPT

A word from Anne Maria's daughter:

'In case, after reading *The Dark Moon*, you are wondering how I feel about it's publication, I want to say that I absolutely endorse it.

If even one person going through what me and my mum experienced - and - if that person, be it another daughter or another mum can be helped to mend their own broken relationship, then I want them to have access to this part of our story - and to know and have hope that even the deepest and most tragic estrangements can be overcome.'

Bath
England
October 2008

ABOUT THE AUTHOR

Anne Maria Clarke is a writer and storyteller working in the field of myth, fairytale and legend. Since 1990 she has adapted numerous stories for cd and live performance, including *The Celtic Quest for the Grail*, *The Sleeping Beauty*, *The Six Swans* and the *Egyptian myth of Isis and Osiris*.

In *The Dark Moon* she draws upon this experience, using extracts from her previous works, in order to bring meaning and understanding to the issue of loss and recovery in her own personal life.

The extracts from her previous works are high-lighted throughout the book in a separate font called:

Faerie

BIBLIOGRAPHY

Baring, Anne & Jules Cashford, *Myth of the Goddess: Evolution of an Image*. London: Arkana, Penguin, 1993

Chetwynd, Tom, *A Dictionary of Symbols*. London: Grafton Books, Collins Publishing Group, 1982

Eliot, T. S.1940, *The Wasteland and Other Poems*. London: Faber & Faber, 1999

Eliot, T. S.1944, *Four Quartets*. London: Faber & Faber, 2000

Estes, Clarissa Pinkola, *Women who Run with the Wolves*. London: Rider, Random House Group, 1992

Frankel: Richard, *The Adolescent Psyche: Jungian and Winicottian Perspectives*. London: Routledge, 1998

Gitanjali, in Rabindranath Tagore, *Song Offerings*. London: Papermac, Macmillan, 1986

Hall, Nor, *The Moon and the Virgin: Reflections on the Archetypal Feminine*. London: Women's Press, 1980

Jones, Gwyn & Thomas Jones, tr., *The Mabonogian,* Manchester: C. Nichols and Company, 1978

Lawrence, D. H., 'The Song of the Man that Came Through' in *The Complete Poems of D. H. Lawrence*. London: Wordsworth, 1994

Matthews, Caitlin, *Sophia: Goddess of Wisdom*. London: Mandala, Harper-Collins, 1991. Quest 2001.

Matthews, John, *The Elements of the Grail Tradition*.
Shaftbury, Element Books, 1978

Mayne, Michael, *Learning to Dance*.
Darton, Longman & Todd, 2001

Nauman, Emil 1882, tr. F. Praeger, *History of Music*. London

Ashcroft-Nowiki, Dolores, *First Steps in Ritual: Magical Techniques for Experiencing the Inner Worlds*.
Wellingborough: Aquarian Press, Thorsons, 1990

Rudhayer, Dane, *The Lunation Cycle: Key to the Understanding of Personality*. USA: Aurora Press, 1971

Tagore, Rabindranath, *Song Offerings*.
London: Papermac, Macmillan,1986

Winnicott, in Richard Frankel, *The Adolescent Psyche: Jungian and Winicottian Perspectives*.
London: Routledge, 1998